Polka Dot Girls

Designed. Original. Treasured.

By
Kristie Kerr & Paula Yarnes

Contents

Dedication

Dedicated to the girls who inspire us:

Anja who does funny accents...

JoJo who defies all odds...

Catelyn who is a SURVIVOR...

Lucy who LOVES unconditionally...

Betty who LIGHTS UP THE ROOM...

Dottie who loves tutus AND fishing poles...

Meg who is so funny she could possibly be the next Lucille Ball...

Ling who is NOT AFRAID to speak her mind...

Natalie who can organize like nobody's business...

Jeorgia who has AMAZING COURAGE...

and **Lily** who is simply sweet!

You amaze us.
Go change the world.

We Need Each Other

WHAT'S THE POINT?

GOD CREATED US TO SHARE OUR LIVES WITH OTHER PEOPLE.

theme verse

Treat people in the same way that you want them to treat you.

Luke 6:31 (CEB)

related bible story

God gives Adam a companion

Genesis 2

It's not very much fun being by yourself. Can you imagine what it would be like if you didn't have any friends or family? I don't think that would be very much fun at all!

God made us with a desire for relationships. There is something inside of us that needs to have other people in our lives.

The Bible tells us that God created everything – the entire universe and everything in it was created by Him! But that wasn't His greatest creation. Oh no… the greatest thing God made was US! The Bible tells us that the first person God created was a man named Adam. He was the very first person on the earth. Genesis 2:7 says, *"Then the Lord God formed the man from the dust of the ground. He breathed the breath of life into the man's nostrils, and the man became a living person."*

1

Adam lived in the beautiful Garden of Eden. It had everything he could have ever wanted inside of it. But one thing was missing: Someone with whom Adam could share his life. In Genesis 2:18, God said, "*It is not good for the man to be alone.*" God knew that we needed other people in our lives to talk to, encourage and support, and to be there for one another.

So God made beautiful Eve, the very first woman. (Girls Rock!!) Not only was she Adam's wife – she was Adam's friend. The Bible calls her Adam's helper or companion. A companion is someone who is by your side as you go on a journey. God gave Adam a companion to walk with him through life. No matter what was going to happen in Adam's life, he now had someone who would be alongside him!

Isn't that cool! Out of all the cool things that God gives us (and He gives us LOTS of really cool things) friendship and companionship are one of His best ideas! God doesn't make us go through life all by ourselves. He gives us family and friends, pastors and teachers, neighbors and classmates to share our lives with us.

I am so thankful for all the relationships that God has given to me. I am thankful for my Mom and Dad who have loved me and taken good care of me. I am thankful for the friends that God has given me who make me laugh and listen to me cry. I am thankful for teachers who have taught me how to do things and helped me learn all kinds of important stuff. (Yes… even the MATH teachers… even though I REALLY hated math class!!!)

God doesn't want us to go through life by ourselves. He KNOWS that it is not good for us to be alone, so He gives us people to share our lives. I know that sometimes it can feel like you are all alone, but the truth is that God has provided LOTS of people who care about you, love you, and want to be your companion as you grow and learn about life.

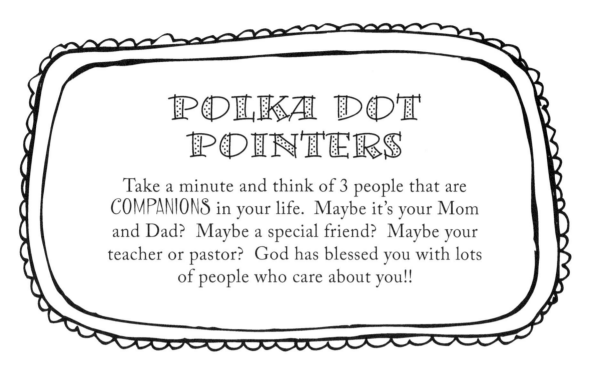

POLKA DOT POINTERS

Take a minute and think of 3 people that are COMPANIONS in your life. Maybe it's your Mom and Dad? Maybe a special friend? Maybe your teacher or pastor? God has blessed you with lots of people who care about you!!

God blesses us by giving us people in our lives. They are a gift to us. And just like any gift we are given, we need to appreciate it and take care of it. We need to be thankful for the friends and family God has given us and make sure we work really hard at being a good friend, daughter, student, classmate, and family member.

But let's be really honest. Our relationships are one of our greatest blessings, but they can also be one of our biggest problems! We can have fights with our friends. Our brothers can pick on us. We can get frustrated with our parents. Our teachers can make us mad and our neighbors can hurt our feelings.

God knows how important your relationships are to you, and so He wants to help you with them! The Bible is full of instructions to help us work out all the problems in our relationships. There are things that God tells us to do to be a good friend. He shows us what kind of attitude we should have toward our parents. He helps us by showing us how to treat people who aren't kind and loving to us. God wants to help you with your relationships!

No matter what kind of questions you have about your relationships, God has the answers. He promises to help you with **ALL** the relationships in your lives because He knows how important they are.

In this book, we are going to take a look at all the relationships in our lives. We are going to check out what the Bible has to say about being a good friend. We are going to learn how to treat the people around us and how to behave in order to take really, really good care of all the relationships God has given to us.

God gives us really specific ideas as to how we can take care of our relationships, but there is one scripture in the Bible that will be our theme throughout the next few weeks. It is a magic secret weapon that you can use in ANY relationship, at ANY time, ANY place – no matter what the situation may be. Are you ready? Do you want to hear God's magic super secret weapon for having good relationships?

Ok……. Here it is……… are you SURE you're ready? Cause it's a REALLY big deal. Ok……… I think you're ready now.

Treat people in the same way that you want them to treat you.
Luke 6:31 (CEB)

It seems pretty simple, right? Treat other people the way YOU want to be treated. Any time you are faced with a situation and you wonder what you should say or do, all you have to do is ask yourself the question, "How would I want someone to treat ME if I was in the same situation?" and you'll have your answer.

We should treat people the way we want to be treated. If you are wondering if you should say something, ask yourself how you would feel if someone said that exact same thing about YOU. If you are wondering if you should do something, ask yourself how you would feel if someone did the same thing to you.

God wants you to treat other people the way you want to be treated. When you do this, your relationships will grow stronger. And strong relationships are super important because they are such a valuable part of our life.

Here are 3 reasons why your relationships are so important!

⟹ 1. Your relationships help you grow.

Sheila never really felt like she was good at anything. While her friends were getting better at tennis and playing the piano, Sheila simply watched from the sidelines. She really wanted to be good at something, but she just couldn't seem to find the thing that made her heart sing.

But when she started third grade, she had a new teacher named Mrs. Schneider. Mrs. Schneider seemed to see something in Sheila that she had never seen in herself. She noticed that Sheila really enjoyed the times in class where they got to work on computers. So one day, she asked Sheila to create a special presentation for the class.

Sheila found herself super nervous about the project, but also super excited too! The more she worked on the project, the more she realized how much she really enjoyed creating things on the computer. It came really easy to her, and she found herself working for hours without even noticing!

When Sheila grew up, she got a job working with computers! She loves her work and is really, really good at it. There are many times when she thinks about Mrs. Schneider who helped her discover her love of computers. She often wonders if she would be doing what she is doing without the encouragement and support that Mrs. Schneider gave her in the third grade.

God will bring people into your life that will help you grow! He will use them to show you new things, inspire you to try something different, and even help you find your gifts and talents. You will have friends who will cheer you on as you discover the things you are good at. You have family members who will help you see something in yourself that you may have never seen on your own. God uses other people to help us grow in all kinds of areas of our lives!

The second reason relationships are so important is:

➡ **2. Your relationships help you rub off the rough edges.**

Katie had developed a bad habit. When other people were trying to tell her a story, she would interrupt them. She wasn't trying to be rude, she would just think of what she wanted to say and blurt it out without thinking.

One day, her very best friend in the whole wide world, Nicki, was telling her something when she once again jumped in and interrupted. Nicki took a deep breath and gently stopped her and said, "Katie, I was telling you a story and you stopped and interrupted me. You are my best friend, but it really hurts my feelings when you do that."

At first, Katie was mad! "I don't do that!" she thought to herself! But then she realized that Nicki was right… she really hadn't been listening and had rudely interrupted her friend. She had a decision to make right then. She could get upset at Nicki and storm off, or she could admit that she had gotten into a bad habit and listen to her friend.

"I'm sorry," Katie said. "I shouldn't have interrupted you. Please finish your story."

We ALL have things we need to work on in our lives. NONE of us are perfect, and there are always areas of our lives where we can get rid of some stuff that isn't the best.

And MANY times, God will use the other people in our lives to help us see things that we need to work on. And even though it can be hard to take sometimes, knowing that our friends love us and want to help us makes all the difference. Proverbs 27:6 tells us, *"Wounds from a sincere friend are better than many kisses from an enemy."* What that means is, even though it's never fun to hear things that we are doing wrong, we can trust that our friends want to help us. We can trust that when they tell us something, they are doing it out of love because they want the best for us.

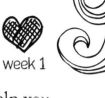

A good friend will help you stop a bad habit. Your Mom and Dad can help you get over a behavior that isn't good so that you don't hurt other people by your actions. A teacher can show you how to overcome a problem and figure out a new way to do things.

Have you ever used sandpaper before? It is a really stiff piece of paper that is covered in hundreds of little pieces of grainy material that makes it really rough. When you rub it over a piece of wood, the rough stuff on the sandpaper rubs away all the rough parts of the wood. After a while, the wood will be smooth and it won't have any more slivers or bad spots… it will be nice and clean.

And a good friend is JUST like sandpaper! They help rub away all your rough edges and help you get past the things you do that could hurt other people by lovingly showing you how to be a better friend!

As iron sharpens iron, so a FRIEND sharpens a FRIEND.
– Proverbs 27:17

So, your relationships help you grow, your relationships help rub off the rough edges of your life, and lastly:

⇒ 3. Your relationships help you through hard stuff.

Kara was going through a tough time with her family. Her parents were fighting a lot and her brother and sister were really busy with all of their friends and activities. Kara felt so lonely and sad, and she wasn't sure what to do.

One day her friend Kelsey noticed that something was wrong. She asked Kara if she was ok, and suddenly everything that had been weighing on Kara's heart came rushing out. She told Kara all the things she was feeling and how worried she was about everything. As she shared what was going on in her life, suddenly the weight that had been on her didn't seem quite so heavy anymore.

The people in your life can help get you through the hard things that we all face. Your parents can help you work through a tough season with your friends. Your teachers can help you overcome some fears you might have at school. Your friends can stand beside you when you are facing all kinds of things and remind you that you are not alone. Proverbs 17:17 says, *"A FRIEND is always loyal, and a brother is born to help in time of need."*

God doesn't want us to go through life alone. He gave us other people to walk through our lives together. It is one of His best gifts and we want to make sure we take really, really good care of it.

Closing Prayer: *Dear God, Thank you for the amazing gift of relationships. Thank you that you have blessed me with friends and family who will walk through my life with me. Help me to treat people the way I want to be treated, and take good care of all the relationships in my life. I love you. Amen.*

God said, "*It is not good for man to be alone.*" So he made a companion for Adam. What is a companion? Write out some ideas here.

God brings all kinds of special people into our lives. Think about someone who is very special to you. Why is that person important to you? Cut out some pictures of that person and glue them here. Also write out some of the reasons that person is special to you in fun colors!

Our theme verse for the week is "*Treat people in the same way that you want them to treat you.*" – Luke 6:31. Think of some ways that you want people to treat you and write out those words here. (Example: kind, patient, friendly)

God gives us relationships to help us grow! In the center of each flower, write the name of a person who has helped you and the thing that they helped you with!

Our relationships can help us "rub off the rough edges of our lives." Ask your mom or dad to give you a piece of sandpaper and glue it here. Then write out the verse: *As iron sharpens iron, so a friend sharpens a friend.* – Proverbs 27:17

God uses other people to help us during hard times. Have you ever had someone help you when you were sad, afraid, or nervous about something? How did they help you?

Help Me Grow Thumbprint T-shirt

<u>Supplies Needed:</u>

- White t-shirt
- Cardboard
- Yellow fabric paint for the center of the flowers
- Variety of pretty color fabric paints for the flowers
- Green fabric marker
- Paper Plates

<u>What Should I Do Next?</u>

- Cut a piece of cardboard to fit inside your t-shirt, separating the front and the back.

- Squeeze a small amount of yellow and your favorite color fabric paint onto a paper plate.

- Dip a pinky finger into the yellow paint and press it onto the t-shirt to create a flower center. Repeat this step to create as many flowers as you want.

- Next, dip a thumb into a different color of paint and press it onto the shirt around the yellow center to create petals. Repeat this step for each flower.

- With a green fabric marker create a stem and leaves for each flower.

- **Important!** With the green fabric marker write the name of each person who has helped you grow.

- Leave the cardboard inside the shirt while it dries and refer to the fabric paint bottle for washing instructions.

Activity Sheets

God created us to share our lives with other people. In the frames, draw and color the following pictures:

You and your parents

You and your favorite teacher

You and your best friend

The first two companions on Earth: Adam & Eve

Find the highlighted words in each verse in the puzzle below. All scripture NIV

*"Do to **others** as you **would** have them do to you."* – Luke 6:31

*"The **LORD** God formed the man from the **dust** of the **ground** and **breathed** into his **nostrils** the breath of **life**, and the man became a **living** being."* – Genesis 2:7

*"The LORD **God** said, "It is not **good** for the man to be **alone**. I will make a **helper** suitable for him."* – Genesis 2:18

*"**Wounds** from a **friend** can be **trusted**, but an enemy multiplies **kisses**."* – Proverbs 27:6

*"As **iron** sharpens iron, so one man **sharpens** another."* – Proverbs 27:17

```
D D L M T B D G Y T G O L U A
R K E C K N K R W E O G N T S
O E H T E Z S O T R D S I N A
L T Y I S G U U L Z A X E L S
K I R J M U A N K A C P V C B
Y F R S X U R D S E R E H V R
B Q L O M E K T X A W F I L E
X J X O N M N I H R A I B E A
Q R N O U M S S S N E L M R T
V T L W J F O W E S S P Y N H
E A U S Q V R F O R E N L V E
S L I R T S O N E U P S U E D
L I V I N G E H D H L U S H H
C L G O O D T A Q Z O D P B U
I F Y P N O G D U S T X V D Y
```

Step 1: Read each verse below and find the missing word. All scripture NIV

"Do to (1) _____ as you would have them do to you." – Luke 6:31

"The LORD God formed the man from the dust of the ground and breathed into his nostrils the (2) _____ of life, and the man became a living being." – Genesis 2:7

"The LORD God said, "It is not good for the man to be (3) _____. I will make a helper suitable for him." – Genesis 2:18

"Wounds from a friend can be (4) _____, but an enemy multiplies kisses." – Proverbs 27:6

"As iron (5) _____ iron, so one man sharpens another." – Proverbs 27:17

Step 2: Fill in the missing word from each scripture above with the corresponding number.

1. _____   2. _____   5. _____

     _____   _____   _____

     _____   _____   _____

     _____   _____   _____

     _____   _____   4. _____   _____

     _____   _____   3. _____   _____   _____

                               _____   _____   _____

                               _____   _____   _____

                               _____   _____

                               _____

Step 3: Complete the sentence below by copying the letters of the outlined word in Step 2, to discover what God wants us to do with our lives.

God created us to ____ ____ ____ ____ ____ our lives with other people.

Weekly Challenge

Grow – Read the story of God creating Adam and Eve found in Genesis 2.

Love – Think of the people in your life who are important to you. Write them a note or just tell them how much they mean to you. You will make their day!

Act – If you notice someone who seems sad or lonely or upset, go and talk to them. Maybe they just need someone to listen and remind them that they are not alone.

Memorize – Memorize this week's verse.

"Treat people in the same way that you want them to treat you."

Luke 6:31 (CEB)

Friendship

WHAT'S THE POINT?

IF WE WANT TO **HAVE** GOOD FRIENDS, THEN WE MUST **BE** A GOOD FRIEND.

theme verse

"A man that hath friends must show himself friendly..."
Proverbs 18:24 (KJ21)

related bible story

Ruth and Naomi
Ruth 1

There's NOTHING like a really good friend. You know, the kind that you can laugh with until your face hurts and your stomach aches. The kind that you can talk to on your very worst day and they somehow make you feel better. The kind that just KNOWS when you are super nervous about your school project and they can make you feel like everything is going to be OK.

Good friends are gifts from God. He loves to bless us with people who make our lives better. God gives us friends so we have can have fun together! He gives us friends to support and encourage us when we're going through hard times. He gives us friends to challenge us and inspire us to grow. And God gives us friends so we know we're not alone in this life.

When I think of all the friends that God has given me, I am amazed at how many of them there are and how each one brings such unique and fun things to my life. There is my friend Jessica who is SO smart – she inspires me to work hard and learn new things. My friend Dawn is such an encourager – she always sends me sweet notes and emails that make me feel good about myself. My friend Diane is so much fun – she always knows how to make me laugh. My friend Jen is so loyal – I know that I can count on her for anything. And my friend Brenda is a huge help to me – anytime I need something, she is always willing to lend me a hand.

Our friendships are something that we should take really good care of. The Bible tells that if we want to HAVE good friends, then we must BE a good friend. Proverbs 18:24 says, *"A man that hath friends must show himself friendly…"* (KJ21) This means that we need to take the time and effort to make sure that we are being a good friend.

Remember God's super-secret weapon for relationships?!?? Treat other people the way you want to be treated! So you should BE the kind of friend that you would want to have!!!

So, what are some ways that we can be a good friend?

➡ 1. Be a LOYAL friend.

What does it mean to be loyal? A loyal friend is someone you can count on. It's someone who you KNOW will be there for you no matter what. It is someone who has your back no matter what you may face.

Being loyal means that your friends know that they can count on you. If something is going on in their lives, they know that you will be there for them. If other people are saying bad things about you, a loyal friend will stick up for you. No matter what, you are confident that they have your back.

Have you ever had a really loyal friend? Someone who was always there for you no matter what? There is nothing quite as comforting as knowing that there is someone sticking up for you. It is such a good feeling to know that there are people who will always be there for you and who are willing to stand up to other people for you.

Have you ever had a friend who wasn't loyal? The kind of friend who will be your friend one day and then the next day they will be mad at you? Or maybe you have had a friend who says, "I'm not going to be your friend anymore" if you don't do what they want you to do. Loyal friends don't say "I'm not going to be your friend anymore." Loyal friends may have disagreements, but they never threaten to take away their friendship.

I remember a friend that I had when I was younger who was NOT a very loyal friend. It seemed like she was always mad at me for one reason or another. I was never totally sure that she wasn't talking about me behind my back. It took me a long time to realize it, but she wasn't a very good friend to me. After a lot of tears and frustration, I finally decided to spend my time on the friends who were loyal to me. I was still kind to her, and I would still be her friend, but I learned that she just couldn't be a really close friend to me because I couldn't count on her to be there for me.

Maybe you haven't been a very loyal friend. Maybe you haven't been consistent with the friends in your life. Today is the day that you can start being a loyal friend. Decide that you are going to be there for your friends no matter what. When you get frustrated with them, talk it through, but never threaten to take your friendship away. Fill your friends with the confidence that comes from knowing that you'll be there for them.

God wants you to be a LOYAL friend. Proverbs 17:7 says, "*A friend is always loyal.*" If you want to be a good friend, be a loyal friend.

The second way we can be a good friend is to:

→ 2. Be an encourager

Have you ever had a friend in your life that made you feel like you could do anything? You know, the kind that tells you to GO FOR IT and cheers you on along the way? An encouraging friend is someone who helps you believe in yourself. They are the friends who tell you all the things you are good at. They complement you and are proud of you when you do well at something.

Sarah had the most encouraging friend EVER! Her name was Abby. No matter what she was doing, Abby was always there for her. When Sarah decided to audition for the jazz band at school, she was SO nervous she could hardly stand it. But Abby called her and TOTALLY encouraged her. She said, "Sarah, you are SO good – you are going to do AWESOME at your audition. I know you are going to be amazing!" Sarah couldn't believe how much stronger she felt after her friend spoke encouraging words to her.

1 Thessalonians 5:11 says, "*So encourage each other and build each other up.*" God wants us to make each other feel better about ourselves. We should be pointing out all the GOOD things about our friends and encouraging them!

But sometimes it can be hard to be encouraging. Why is that? Sometimes, when our friends do really well at something, we can feel jealous. Or when our friends do something really amazing, it makes us feel bad about ourselves because WE didn't do something as amazing as them. But those are all silly reasons not to encourage our friends, right?!

The truth is, just because someone else is successful doesn't mean that WE won't be successful too! Seeing our friends do well should be something that fills us with joy, not jealousy. Helping our friends feel better about themselves is an awesome thing to do!

Be an encourager. When you notice a friend doing something well, tell them! When someone is nervous about trying something new, tell them that you believe in them and they can do it! Be your friend's biggest supporter and cheerleader.

Encourage each other. Live in harmony and peace.
Then the God of love and peace will be with you.

2 Corinthians 13:11

So, be a good friend by being loyal, encouraging, and lastly,

⇒ 3. Don't be a selfish friend.

Oh my, it can be SO easy to think about the things WE want! The things WE want to play. The things WE want to do. The things WE want our friends to do. The things WE DON'T want our friends to do.

But a good friend doesn't just think about the things WE want, we think about our friends! Philippians 2:3 says, "*Don't be selfish; don't try to impress others. Be humble, thinking of others as better than yourselves.*" This means that we aren't supposed to only think about the things WE want, but we should think about our friends too!

There is a story in the Bible about a girl who did something AMAZINGLY unselfish for her friend. Her name was Ruth, and she was a very good friend to her mother-in-law Naomi. All of Naomi's family had died, so she decided to move away from where she was living, back to the home of her ancestors. Her daughter-in-law, Ruth, decided to go with her so she wouldn't be alone.

Now this was a HUGE deal. Ruth would have to leave all her family and friends and move to a new country where she didn't know anyone! But she knew that her mother-in-law would really need her, and so she was willing to go with her. She thought about Naomi's feelings and needs far above her own. In Ruth 1:16 she says, "*Wherever you go, I will go; wherever you live, I will live. Your people will be my people and your God will be my God.*"

I can imagine that it would have been a difficult decision for Ruth. But she thought about what was best for Naomi and how she could help and support her instead of what might be easiest for her. Ruth was a very unselfish friend.

God wants you to think about other people's feelings – not just your own. He wants you to consider ways that you can encourage and bless the people in your life – not just think about what YOU want all the time.

21

Don't you think it would be so cool if we all could simply be the kind of friend that we would want to have? A friend who is loyal no matter what? A friend who encourages us and cheers us on? And a friend who isn't selfish but thinks of what is best for the other people in their lives?

I want those kinds of friends. And I want to be that kind of friend.

Closing Prayer: *Dear God. Thank you for the gift of friendship. I pray that you will help me be the best friend possible. Help me be loyal, encouraging, and unselfish to the friends in my life. I love you, Amen.*

My Polka Dot SPOT

Do you have a good friend? Cut out some pictures of her and glue them in the space provided and then write out some of the reasons that she is such a good friend to you!

The Bible tells us that if we want to HAVE good friends, then we must BE a good friend. What are some qualities that you would like to have in a friend? Write out your thoughts here.

A LOYAL friend is someone who sticks by you no matter what. Draw a picture of you and a friend sticking together!

Being a good friend means being an encouraging friend. Write the name of one of your friends in the circle below, and then fill in all the circles around it with things you like about her. What are the things she is good at? Why do you like to spend time with her? After you have written down all the things you love about her – share this page with her. She will be so encouraged when she sees all your kind words!

Have you ever had someone say something encouraging to you? Write out what they said to you and how it made you feel.

God doesn't want us to be a selfish friend. What are some ways that you can think of others instead of yourself?

Friendship Mobile

Supplies Needed:

- Friendship Template
- White or Colored Cardstock/or paper of your choice
- Scissors
- Crayons/Markers
- Self-adhesive jewels and pretty embellishments
- Hole Puncher
- String
- Coat Hanger
- Pictures of friends
- Glue Stick
- Ribbon or yarn to wrap around the hanger (optional)
- Glue gun (optional)

Prep:

- Print template onto paper or cut out templates and trace onto paper of your choice.
- Cut out the flowers and hearts.
- Pre-punch holes at the top of each flower and heart using a hole-puncher.
- Cut four differing lengths of string for each heart.
- Cut one to three differing lengths of string for each flower depending on the number of flowers each girl chooses to have for her mobile.
- Thread a piece of string through each pre-punched heart and flower and tie.

What Should I Do Next?

- Color and decorate each flower with crayons/markers/embellishments.

- With a glue stick, glue a picture of each friend in the center of the flower.

- Order the hearts and flowers across the base of the coat hanger.

- When happy with the arrangement, tie each string to the base of the coat hanger and hang in your room!

- Optional step: Before tying the arrangement to the base of the hanger, you can decorate the hanger with your favorite ribbon or yarn by simply wrapping the ribbon around the entire hanger. When finished wrapping, cut any excess ribbon or yarn and attach to the hanger with a dab of glue from a glue gun.

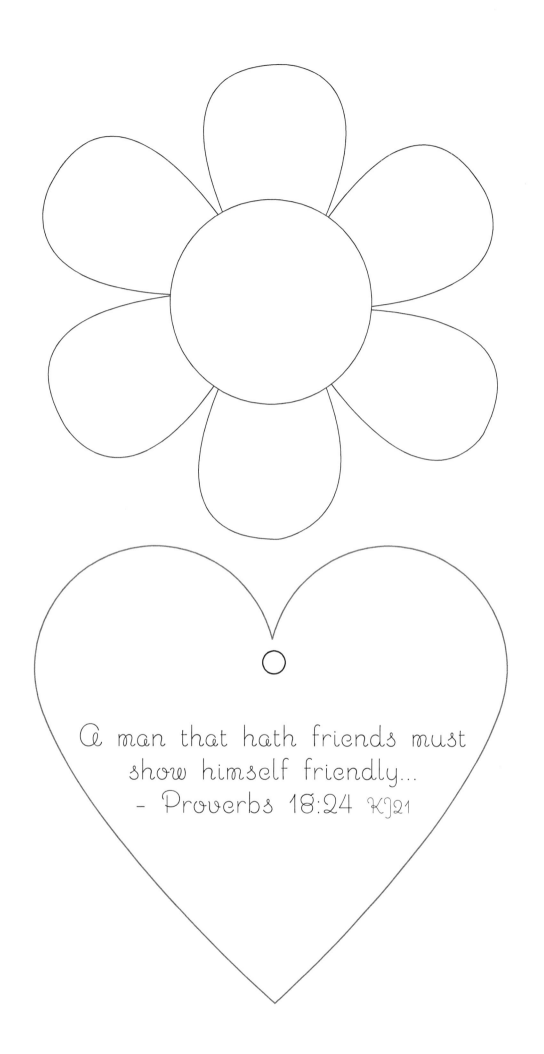

A man that hath friends must
show himself friendly...
- Proverbs 18:24 KJ21

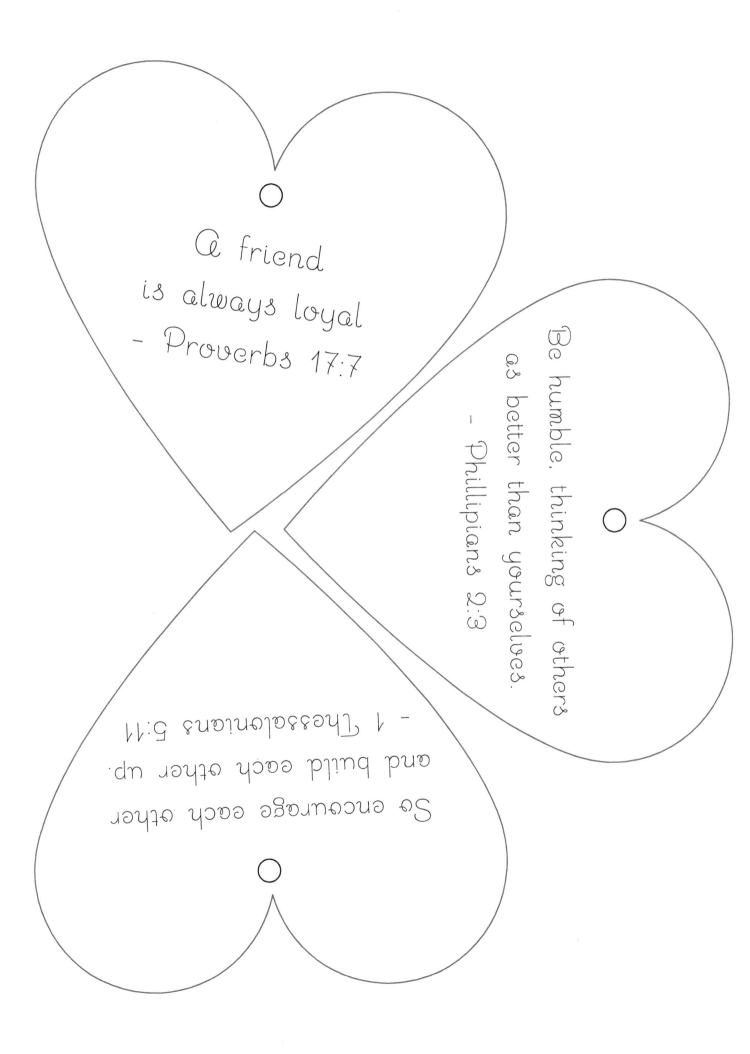

A friend
is always loyal
- Proverbs 17:7

Be humble, thinking of others
as better than yourselves.
- Phillipians 2:3

So encourage each other
and build each other up.
- 1 Thessalonians 5:11

Activity Sheets

Things about us! Fill out this survey with a friend.

Question	Answer: Me	Answer: You
1. Favorite food		
2. Favorite movie		
3. Favorite book		
4. If you could be an animal, what would it be?		
5. What word best describes you?		
6. If you could go anywhere in the world, where would you go?		
7. Name one great thing about your family		
8. Favorite season		
9. Favorite singer		
10. What are you scared of?		

Question	Answer: Me	Answer: You
11. If you won a million dollars, what would you do with it?		
12. Favorite animal		
13. If you could change your name, what would it be?		

14. What do you like better?
    a. Candy or chips
    b. Singing or dancing
    c. Dogs or cats
    d. Sports or music
    e. Shopping or reading
    f. Board games or computer games
    g. Camping or hotels
    h. Sweat pants or jeans
    i. On stage or behind the scenes
    j. Winter or summer
    k. Hot Chocolate or lemonade
    l. Biking or skateboarding		

15. What will I be doing in 10 years?		
16. Will we be friends forever?		

Read the following scriptures about friendship in your Bible and find the missing word. All scripture NIV.

"A friend _____ *at all times."* – Proverbs 17:17

"Perfume and incense bring _____ *to the heart, and the pleasantness of one's friend springs from his earnest counsel."* – Proverbs 27:9

"Live in harmony with one another. Do not be _____, *but be willing to associate with people of low position. Do not be* _____."* – Romans 12:16

"Therefore _____ *one another and build each other up, just as in fact you are doing."* – 1 Thessalonians 5:11

"Do nothing out of _____ *ambition or vain conceit, but in humility consider others better than yourselves."* – Philippians 2:3

WORD LIST

encourage   *conceited*   *joy*   *loves*

selfish   *proud*

Read Ruth 1:16-18 NIV in the Bible and find the missing word. Find those same words in the word search puzzle.

[16]But _____ replied, "Don't urge me to _____ you or to turn back from you. Where you _____ I will go, and where you _____ I will stay. Your _____ will be my people and your _____ my God. [17]Where you _____ I will die, and there I will be _____. May the _____ deal with me, be it ever so severely, if anything but death _____ you and me." [18]When _____ realized that Ruth was _____ to go with her, she stopped urging her.

```
S  E  P  A  R  A  T  E  S  E  O  B
O  L  N  G  B  N  I  O  V  L  L  U
G  P  O  S  T  A  Y  H  D  I  E  R
N  O  D  R  E  O  L  T  O  E  A  I
T  E  D  P  D  M  I  U  M  E  V  E
L  P  D  E  N  I  M  R  E  T  E  D
```

WORD LIST

Ruth	leave	go	Naomi
stay	people	God	determined
buried	Lord	separates	die

Polka Dot Plus

Weekly Challenge

Grow – Read the story of Ruth and Naomi in Ruth chapter 1.

Love – Think of a way you can encourage a friend this week. Send a note, make a phone call, or say something to let your friend know you believe in her!

Act – Do one thing this week to practice being an unselfish friend. Maybe let your friend choose what you do, let her pick first when you're sharing a treat, or simply think of what she would like before you think of what YOU would like.

Memorize – Memorize this week's theme verse.

*"A man that hath friends must show
himself friendly…"*
Proverbs 18:24

My Family

WHAT'S THE POINT?

HONOR YOUR PARENTS, BE KIND TO YOUR FAMILY, AND STICK TOGETHER!

theme verse

*I pray that the Lord will let your family
and your descendants always grow strong.*

Psalm 115:14 CEV

related bible story

Joab and Abishai

I Chronicles 19

They see your best and they know your worst. They are the people who mean the most to you, and the people who can drive you nutty the fastest. The people who you would stick up for to anyone, anywhere, over anything – but also the people who you spend the most time fighting, arguing, and getting crazy mad at. They are the ones who can make you feel the best about yourself, but sometimes they are the people who can say things that make you feel bad, too. Who are these loony people?

Your family.

We talked earlier in this book about the fact that God gives us people in our world to walk through our lives together. And there is NO one closer to us on our journey than our families. They are the ones we live with and spend the most time around.

God gives us families to help us in countless ways. Do you remember being a baby? Really? I don't either. But your parents were the ones who cared for you when you were a baby. They changed your diapers (ick!) and mushed up your food (gross!) and made sure you were taken well care of. As you grew older, they showed you how to do things, taught you all the stuff you needed to learn, and made sure that you were always safe.

And now, your Mom and Dad do their best to teach you all the things you need to learn in order to become the best person you can possibly be. They are not perfect, and will make lots of mistakes, but they love you and want the best for you… even if sometimes they don't do everything perfectly.

And then we have other people in our family! We have brothers and sisters and cousins and grandparents and lots of other people who are all a part of our families. Some people have really big families – and some people have really small families. Some families live really close and spend a lot of time together, and some families don't really spend much time together at all. No matter what your family may look like, God has some instructions for you as to how you should deal with the people in your family.

First of all, God gives us some very important instructions when it comes to how we treat our parents. It is this:

⇒ 1. We need to honor our parents.

There are quite a few places in the Bible where we find this very specific direction. Ephesians 6:1-3 says, " *Children, obey your parents because you belong to the Lord, for this is the right thing to do. Honor your father and mother. This is the first commandment with a promise: If you honor your father and mother, things will go well for you, and you will have a long life on the earth.*"

What does is mean to HONOR our parents? Honoring someone means respecting them. It means obeying them and doing the things that they ask of you. It means speaking to them in a way that isn't sassy or rude. When you honor someone, you are thanking them for the special role that they play in your life.

You see, God has given you to your parents as their responsibility. When you honor them by doing the things they ask of you, speaking in a way that is respectful, and having an attitude of appreciation toward them, you are honoring the role God has given them in your life. So, when you honor your parents, you are really honoring God!

I know that sometimes it can be hard to honor your parents. There are moments when they frustrate us. There are times we simply don't want to do what they say. And sometimes, we don't understand why they want us to do the things they want us to do. But no matter what, you need to HONOR them.

Not only does this please God when we act that way, but there is a reward for us when we follow this very important rule! Actually, this is the first commandment in the Bible that comes with a promise. God makes a deal with us. He says, "If you will honor your parents and treat them with respect, then I am going to help things to go well for you." I think that's a pretty good deal!

You need to work really hard to honor your parents. When you feel like ignoring what they tell you to do, remember that God wants you to honor them by obeying. When you start to say something sassy, stop yourself and remember that God wants you to speak respectfully to your parents. When you are tempted to treat your parents poorly or have a bad attitude, ask God to help you honor your parents even when it is difficult.

Sometimes we can think to ourselves, "Well, I'm frustrated with my Mom and Dad, so I don't have to honor them." You know what? God doesn't tell us that we only honor our parents if we like the things they are telling us to do. He doesn't tell us that we only have to honor our parents when we feel like it. The Bible tells us that it is our responsibility to keep our attitudes respectful and honoring to our parents. It doesn't depend on their behavior toward us, or only if we feel like they have earned it. God wants you to honor your parents, no matter what.

So, God wants you to HONOR your parents.

Just so You Know

There are a lot of situations in which it can be really difficult to honor your parents. Sometimes your parents can go through a hard time and may treat you in a way that they shouldn't. If you are ever scared by something your Mom or Dad are doing, it's really important that you talk to someone about it. Share your concerns with a teacher, another family member, a friend or even your pastor. When you seek help for your Mom or Dad when they need it, you are honoring them in a really special way. You are respecting them enough to get help – and God will be really, really proud of you.

Another thing that God wants you to do is:

⟹ 2. Be KIND to your family.

Kindness, hmmmm. Seems easy enough, right? Of course we all know that we should be kind to each other. But sometimes it can be really hard to be kind to the people closest to us.

Heather has a brother named Joe. Heather loves her brother, but she's not so sure how much she likes him. He can really, really get on her nerves. Sometimes, he does things just to bother her and no matter what she says, he just won't stop. After a while, Heather finds herself EXPLODING at her brother. She screams and yells and sometimes she even wants to hit the little bugger!

What is so crazy is that Heather would NEVER think of screaming or yelling or wanting to hit one of her friends! Even if they made her super mad, she wouldn't think of treating a friend that way.

But sometimes we treat our families way different than we would ever treat our friends. We are a lot less cautious about the things we say and do with the people closest to us. It's easy to forget that our brothers and sisters and other family members have feelings just like our friends!

God wants you to be kind to your family. Even if they are driving you crazy. Even if you are so frustrated you just want to scream! Even if they are not kind to you. 2 Timothy 2:24 says, "*A servant of the Lord must not quarrel but must be kind to everyone, be able to teach, and be patient with difficult people.*" (Yes, your little brother will fall into the category of "difficult people" sometimes!)

You must be kind to your family. Don't say mean things to your brother or sister. Don't tease them. Don't make fun of them. Don't react when they are trying to get you angry. When you feel like you are going to lose it and say something UNKIND, stop yourself and remember that God wants us to be kind to one another. Maybe you'll need to walk away and take a few minutes to calm yourself down. Maybe you need to go talk to your Mom or Dad about the situation. Or maybe you just need to smile at them and tell them you love them.

You will never regret the moments when you are kind to other people. Even if they don't deserve it, you will know that you made the right choice in choosing kindness.

And the last way God wants you to treat your family, is to:

⇒ 3. Stick together.

Remember when we talked about loyalty? Being loyal means you stand by someone no matter what. And there is no place that loyalty is more important than among your family members.

God didn't make a mistake when He put you in the family you are in. He did it for a reason. He gave you your family so you would have someone to walk through life with you… to help you, support you, and have your back.

There is a story in the Bible about two brothers who had each other's backs. Joab was the leader of the army for King David. He had to fight all kinds of bad guys who were trying to destroy the nation of Israel. Joab was facing a tough situation. There were people ahead of him wanting to fight him… and there were people behind him who wanted to fight him. He was surrounded! So you know what he did? He called on his brother to help him. I Chronicles 19:10-13 says, "*When Joab saw that he had two fronts to fight, before and behind, he took his pick of the best of Israel and deployed them to confront the Arameans. The rest of the army he put under the command of Abishai, **his brother**, and deployed them to deal with the Ammonites. Then he said, 'If the Arameans are too much for me, you help me; and if the Ammonites prove too much for you, I'll come and help you. Courage!'*"

Did you read that? These brothers had each others backs! If one of them needed help – they knew that the other one would be there for them. If they were in trouble, their family would fight for them. Joab could confidently go into battle knowing that his brother was right by his side.

We know in our hearts that we should be there for our families. But sometimes we can get so busy with all the things we are doing – our friends, our activities, and the things we are involved in-that we can forget that part of our job is to be there for the people in our families.

Maybe your brother or sister is having a hard time and they don't have anyone to talk to. Would they feel comfortable coming to you with their problems? Would they feel like you would listen to them or help them? Or would they feel like you would tell them to leave you alone so you could do other things?

If your Mom was having a really busy week and she was totally overwhelmed, could she count on you to help her with the chores around the house and to maybe help clean up? Or would you react with a million excuses as to why it's not fair that you have to help.

Families stick together. They help each other out. They work together as a team to help each person succeed.

Have you ever seen someone run a three legged race? It's when they tie two people's legs together and then they try to run while their legs are connected to another person. It is super fun to do – but it is even funnier to watch because most of the time people fall down over and over again!

They fall because each person is trying to run the way they normally run when they're all by themselves. But one person is trying to step forward with their right leg while the other person is trying to step forward with their left leg! Pretty soon they get all their legs tangled up and end up falling flat on their faces.

BUT! If they work together and move their legs at the same time, they can get into a rhythm and eventually they can run as if they were one person!

You see, God wants us to work together with our families as a team. When we try and just do our own things without thinking about the other people in our family, we won't get very far. But if we stop and help each other, and make sure that we all work together, we will be able to run the race of life faster, stronger and more confident than if we were running alone.

Our families are a team. When we only think about ourselves and what we want and what we are doing, we are never going to get anywhere. But when we decide to work together, and think of ways that we can help each other out, our families will grow stronger and we will all be stronger individuals too!

Our families are a gift from God. He blessed you with people who love you, care about you, and want to help you do the very best you can. Don't take your family for granted… but do your best to treat them with all the love and respect you can. Yes… even your annoying little brother.

Closing Prayer: *Dear God, thank you for my family. I know that they are a special treasure from you, and I am so grateful for them. Show me ways that I can honor my Mom and Dad. Help me show kindness to my family members, even when it's hard. And teach me ways that I can support my family and help us work together as a team. I love you, Jesus. Amen.*

My
Polka Dot
SPOT

God gives our families to us as a gift. What are some things that you love about your family? Cut out pictures of your family members, glue them here, and then write out some of your favorite things about them.

_____   _____
_____   _____

_____   _____
_____   _____

What does it mean to honor your parents?

Ephesians 6:1-3 tells us, "*Children, obey your parents because you belong to the Lord, for this is the right thing to do. Honor your father and mother. This is the first commandment with a promise: If you honor your father and mother, things will go well for you, and you will have a long life on the earth.*" God asks us to do something, and then He makes a promise to us. Fill in the blanks below.

If i honor my parents, then things will go _____ for me.

Another thing that God wants us to do is to treat our family with kindness. Why do you think it is so hard to be kind to our family sometimes?

What are some specific ways you can be kind to your family? Write out the name of each family member and then list 3 ways that you can show kindness to them.

Name _____

-
-
-

Name _____

-
-
-

Name _____

-
-
-

Name _____

-
-
-

Name _____

-
-
-

Another way we can be a good member of a family is by sticking together. What does it mean to "have someone's back?"

Draw a picture of you and your family together, supporting each other and having each other's backs!

Plan a Family Fun Night!

Many families are always on the GO. With all the activities that happen during the week, it's hard to fit in time to enjoy each other's company. It is really important to spend at least one night a week doing something together as a family.

So here is a challenge…Surprise your family and plan a super fun night together! Here are some fun ideas to get you started.

Themed Movie Night!
- Create tickets to fit your theme.
- Make your own concession stand and "sell" popcorn and soda.
- Create your own trivia game around the movie.

InterACTIVE Night!
- Play the Wii or Xbox 360.
- Serve healthy snacks.

I'm NOT Board Game Night!
- Play games like Monopoly, Sorry, Battleship, Yahtzee, Uno.
- If you want to get really close, pull out the game Twister.
- Don't forget snacks.

Food, Food and More Food!
- Make dinner together…give each family member a job in the meal preparation so that everyone is included.
- Have a cupcake decorating contest.
- Create a family ice cream sundae…see how high you can pile on the toppings!

To make this night really special, create an invitation for everyone in your family!

Activity Sheets

2 Timothy 2:24 says "*A servant of the Lord must not quarrel but must* BE *kind to everyone,* BE *able to teach, and* BE *patient with difficult people.*"

With a friend or family member, color the bee and create an awesome scene with your best doodles!

God gives us people in our world to walk through our lives together. And there is NO one closer to us on our journey than our families.

Step 1: Read 1 Chronicles 19

Step 2: Find the words from the story in the Word Search Puzzle.

Word Search Puzzle

```
I  P  A  R  A  S  Y  R  T  H  A  T  T  H  G
E  R  P  T  S  S  E  N  D  N  I  K  P  O  P
T  O  P  L  O  S  O  L  R  D  W  A  D  A  I
Y  N  R  R  P  G  L  K  C  I  T  S  R  J  L
L  O  E  E  A  L  E  E  T  I  Y  E  O  O  U
I  H  C  M  R  Y  F  T  E  A  N  A  M  I  L
M  T  I  O  D  Y  A  N  H  T  B  O  N  D  Y
A  Y  A  B  O  N  C  U  S  E  R  D  R  T  E
F  S  T  E  C  E  A  E  N  D  R  A  L  H  N
T  S  E  Y  A  L  W  M  A  Y  S  A  G  R  C
A  B  I  S  H  A  I  O  M  W  Y  S  T  R  O
N  G  L  I  E  J  B  C  K  O  D  O  D  S  M
E  P  S  K  S  M  X  R  L  O  C  E  I  G  Q
N  S  X  Q  B  Z  W  O  F  X  A  M  J  W  H
Q  M  B  B  M  P  X  E  M  B  R  V  Q  G  K
```

Word List

Abishai	*Joab*	*appreciate*	*Chronicles*
commandment	*family*	*God*	*honor*
kindness	*loyalty*	*obey*	*parents*
patience	*pray*	*respect*	*stick*
together			

No matter what your family may look like, God has some instructions for you as to how you should deal with the people in your family.

Step 1: Unscramble the words to reveal God's instructions.

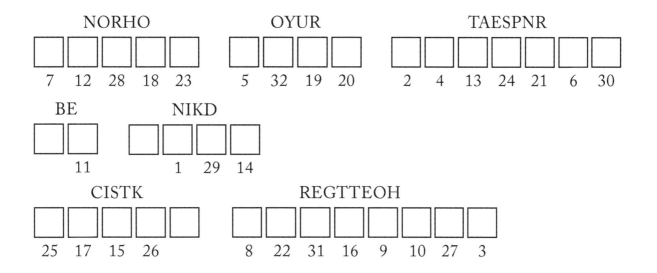

NORHO
7 12 28 18 23

OYUR
5 32 19 20

TAESPNR
2 4 13 24 21 6 30

BE
11

NIKD
1 29 14

CISTK
25 17 15 26

REGTTEOH
8 22 31 16 9 10 27 3

Step 2: Copy the letters in the numbered cells to other cells with the same number to reveal God's Word.

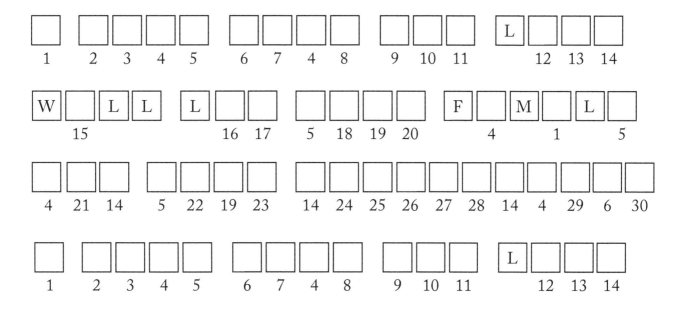

1 2 3 4 5   6 7 4 8   9 10 11   L 12 13 14

W 15   L L   L 16 17   5 18 19 20   F 4   M 1   L 5

4 21 14   5 22 19 23   14 24 25 26 27 28 14 4 29 6 30

1 2 3 4 5   6 7 4 8   9 10 11   L 12 13 14

W □ L L   L □ □   □ □ □ □   F □ M □ L □
 15   16 17   5 18 19 20   4   1   5

□ □ □   □ □ □ □   □ □ □ □ □ □ □ □ □ □ □ □
4 21 14 5 22 19 23 14 24 25 26 27 28 14 4 29 6 30

□ L W □ □ □   □ □ □ W   □ □ □ □ □ □
4   4 5 25   31 3 32   25 6 3 22 21 31

□ □ □ L M   115:14   □ □ V
2 25 4   26 11

Polka Dot Plus

Weekly Challenge

Grow – Read the story of Joab and Abishai in I Chronicles 19.

Love – Think of some things about your family that you are thankful for. Write a note to some of your family members telling them why you are glad God gave them to you.

Act – Practice being kind to your family. When you get frustrated or upset with someone, choose to respond in kindness instead of anger and frustration.

Memorize – Memorize the theme verse.

"I pray that the Lord will let your family and your descendants always grow strong."
Psalm 115:14 CEV

Elders

WHAT'S THE POINT?

GOD HAS PLACED PEOPLE IN AUTHORITY OVER OUR LIVES AND WE NEED TO TREAT THEM WITH HONOR AND RESPECT.

theme verse

For all authority comes from God, and those in positions of authority have been placed there by God.

Romans 13:1

related bible story

Jesus on Authority

Matthew 22:15-21

We have talked a lot so far about the relationships that God brings into our lives to help us. We have talked about friends that come along side of us and are our companions on our journey. We have talked about our families who stand by us and help take care of us. But today we are going to talk about one more group of people who God brings into our world to teach us. They are called "elders."

Now, that is kind of a funny old fashioned word that we don't use very much. But let me tell you who your "elders "are. An elder is anyone older than you, anyone who is in leadership over you, or anyone who has any kind of authority in your life. Let's take a closer look at each of those three areas and see who the "elders" are in your life.

59

First of all, an elder is

➡ 1. Someone OLDER than you.

Can you think of someone in your life who is older than you? Yes, your friend down the street may be two months older than you, but that doesn't necessarily make her your elder. What I'm talking about is someone who is a few years older than you or an adult. It could be your parents, grandparents, aunt and uncle, teacher, or simply someone walking on the street that is older than you. Those people are your elders because they were born before you.

We are supposed to honor the people who are older than us. They have experienced lots of things in their lives that you haven't experienced yet, and God wants you to honor them with your words, actions, and attitude. When you honor them, you are recognizing that they know things you don't know and that you respect their position.

Caroline was getting on a bus at the airport to go on vacation with her family. The bus was really crowded and there were only a few more seats available. Caroline had just settled into her seat when a woman who looked about the age of her grandmother walked onto the bus. There were no seats left, and the woman was left standing in the middle of the aisle. As soon as Caroline's Dad noticed the woman standing there, he jumped up and offered his seat to the older woman. She thanked him and quietly slipped into her father's seat.

After they got off the plane, Caroline asked her Dad a question. "Dad, why did you give that woman your seat on the bus?" "Well," her Dad replied, "it is a way that I honor her because she is older than me. It was something I could do to show her respect."

There are lots of ways that we can honor the older people in our lives. Caroline's Dad showed us a HUGE way – and that is by doing kind things for people older than us. Offering them our seat, opening a door for them, helping them carry something to their car… these are all ways in which we can show respect for someone older than us.

Another way you can honor your elders is by being kind and nice to people who are older. Sometimes younger people don't really appreciate people who are older than them. They can ignore them or sometimes even make fun of them. But that is not at all the kind of attitude God wants you to have toward people older than you. God wants you to honor and respect the elders in your life simply because they have gone before you and have wisdom and experiences that you can learn from!

1 Peter 5:5 says, "*In the same way, you younger men must accept the authority of the elders. And all of you, serve each other in humility, for God opposes the proud but favors the humble.*" God wants you to have a humble, serving heart toward the older people in your life. This attitude pleases God and He will bless you for your sweet heart towards your elders.

The second group of people that are your elders are

➡ 2. Those who are in LEADERSHIP over you.

Irene was really excited to join the book club her local library was starting. She was so looking forward to spending time with other girls who loved to read as much as she did and discussing all her favorite books.

The first day of book club she met Stacy, who was the leader of the group. Stacy was only a couple of years older than Irene, but the librarian had put her in charge of the group. Irene instantly knew that Stacy was going to get on her nerves. She was kind of a know-it-all and never really gave the other girls in the group a chance to talk. She was also pretty bossy and set up a whole lot of rules and guidelines as to how the book club was going to run.

Every time Irene would head to the library for book club, she would start to get frustrated. She thought to herself, "I could do a way better job leading the group than Stacy is." She would think negatively about Stacy and her silly rules and super smarty pants attitude.

One day, she decided to talk to her Mom about the book club situation. She explained her frustrations about Stacy and waited for her mother's advice. Her Mom listened closely and then took a deep breath and gave Irene some important advice.

"You know honey, I know that sometimes it's difficult to be in a group where the leader does things differently than you would do them. I have been in the same position many times myself. But, as long as you are a part of the group, you need to honor Stacy's leadership. You can do that by keeping a good attitude, trying to follow the rules and guidelines that she has set up, and by keeping your words and actions kind and loving even when you are frustrated."

This wasn't exactly the answer that Irene was hoping for. She wanted her Mom to say that if Stacy was bugging her so much, then she should just quit the group or tell her that she didn't like the way she was doing things. But her Mom was trying to teach her a very important lesson: it's important that we honor people who are in leadership over us even if we don't always like or agree with the way they are leading.

You see, the Bible tells us that ANYONE who is in ANY position of leadership over us has been put there by God. SERIOUSLY! Anyone who is a teacher, leader, mentor, or any other position of leadership in your life has been put there by God because He wants you to learn something from them. Sometimes we can forget that – especially if we're frustrated with our teacher, small group leader, student council president, or anyone else who is your leader.

But God tells us specifically how we should treat people who are in leadership over us. Romans 13:1 tells us, "*Everyone must submit to governing authorities. For all authority comes from God, and those in positions of authority have been placed there by God.*" God has put them in their place, and so our attitude should be respectful.

When you honor the leaders in your life, you are really saying, "God, I trust that you put this person in my life to teach me something." Perhaps God has given you a leader who will show you how to be kind and treat people well. Maybe God has given you a leader that can teach you special knowledge and insight

they may have. Or maybe they have a specific skill or talent that they can help you grow or develop.

And sometimes, God allows us to be under a leader who simply shows us the way NOT to do things. No matter what, our response to people in leadership should be one of respect.

Irene decided to be the best book club member she could possibly be, even though it was really hard sometimes. She decided to honor the commitment she made to be in the group and not to quit. She respectfully followed the rules that Stacy set up, and when she made suggestions as to how to make the group better, she did so in a respectful and humble attitude.

When the year ended, the librarian called her up and asked her if SHE would be interested in leading the group for the next year. Hmmmmmmm….Very interesting!

Do you know what? Irene was very excited to lead the group, and she knew EXACTLY the way she was going to lead the group. She knew that she wanted to give the other girls plenty of time to share their opinions because she knew how frustrating it was when Stacy dominated the conversation. She knew she wanted guidelines, but she approached the rules of the club differently than Stacy did because of her own experience.

Irene realized that God had rewarded her decision to honor the leader that He had put over her. She knew there were a lot of things that she had learned from Stacy that were really helpful when it came time for HER to lead the group. And she was especially thankful that she had been respectful of Stacy when she was in charge, because this was the kind of attitude she wanted the members of her group to have toward her now. (Remember?!?!? Super-secret special weapon?!? Treat others the way you want to be treated?!??!)

God will put hundreds of people in leadership over you during your lifetime. You can make a decision right now to be respectful, honoring, and someone with a good attitude to all the people in leadership over you.

So, God wants us to honor people older than us, people in leadership over us, and lastly, God wants us to honor

➡3. People in AUTHORITY over us.

Who is an authority in your life? Basically, it's anyone who has the power to get you into trouble. Your parents are your authority. Your teachers and principals are your authority. Your grandparents and aunts and uncles are your authority. The policemen in your town are your authority. Even the president is an authority over you!

1 Peter 2:13-14 tells us, "*For the Lord's sake, respect all human authority—whether the king as head of state, or the officials he has appointed.*" God puts people in positions of authority in our families, communities, cities, and even our country. They are in the positions they are in because God has placed them there for a specific plan and purpose.

We are supposed to respect those people by honoring them with our attitude, speaking respectfully about them with our words, and by obeying the rules they put over us.

Sometimes we don't agree with everything the people in authority over us think or believe, but God still wants us to respect and honor them. It can be really easy to get frustrated and disappointed in the way some leaders behave, but God tells us that we should pray for them and maintain a respectful attitude even in our disagreement with them.

Jesus actually was caught in a situation where some people were trying to get him to say something bad about the people in authority over him. During the days when Jesus was teaching on the earth, the people in charge of the government were the Romans and they were led by a man named Caesar. Now, they were not leaders who honored God. Actually, they kind of looked at their country as a god. They wanted people to worship them and didn't like it when the people served God.

There were also some religious leaders who didn't like Jesus. They were trying to find ways to get Him in trouble and to make Him look bad in front of other people. So, one day, they asked Him a question in front of the crowds.

Matthew 22:15-21 says, *"Then the Pharisees met together to plot how to trap Jesus into saying something for which he could be arrested. They sent some of their disciples, along with the supporters of Herod, to meet with him. "Teacher," they said, "We know how honest you are. You teach the way of God truthfully. You are impartial and don't play favorites. Now tell us what you think about this: Is it right to pay taxes to Caesar or not?"*

But Jesus knew their evil motives. "You hypocrites!" he said. "Why are you trying to trap me? Here, show me the coin used for the tax." When they handed him a Roman coin, he asked, "Whose picture and title are stamped on it?"

"Caesar's," they replied.

"Well, then," he said, "give to Caesar what belongs to Caesar, and give to God what belongs to God."

His reply amazed them, and they went away."

You see, the religious leaders were hoping to get Jesus to say something bad about the government and people in authority over the area where He was living. But Jesus refused to do it. He chose to honor the authority that God has placed over Him, even though He didn't like A LOT of the things they were saying and doing. He recognized the importance of honoring the authority God had place in leadership at the time.

You can honor those in authority in your life by speaking respectfully about them. You can honor the authority in your life by following the rules and laws of the land. And you can especially honor authority by praying for them and doing everything you can to be a Godly influence and example to all the people you come into contact with.

God wants you to be respectful of your elders. It pleases His heart when you honor those in leadership over you.

You know why?

Cause when you respect the elders in your life you are really respecting God. You are acknowledging that He is in charge of everything and that you trust that He is simply putting you right where you need to be. You are trusting His plan for your life. You are saying that you believe that He is in control even if you don't always understand how or why He is doing the things He is doing.

Honor the authority in your life. Sometimes it is hard, but God will help you have the right attitude. He will help you be a good example to others of what it means to live a life that belongs to Jesus.

Closing Prayer: *Dear God. I want to honor you by honoring the elders in my life. Help me to treat the older people in my life with dignity and respect. Show me how I can support and learn from people who You have put in leadership over my life. And I pray for the people in authority in my school, city, and country. I pray that you would give them wisdom and teach me how to have a respectful and helpful attitude toward them. I love you, Jesus, Amen.*

My
Polka Dot
SPOT

An "elder" is someone older than you, someone in leadership over you, and someone who is an authority in your life.

Who are some people in your life who are older than you? Write their names here or better yet, cut out some pictures and glue them here!

What are some ways that you can honor and respect elders in your life?

Who are some of the people in leadership in your life? Write their names in the circles below.

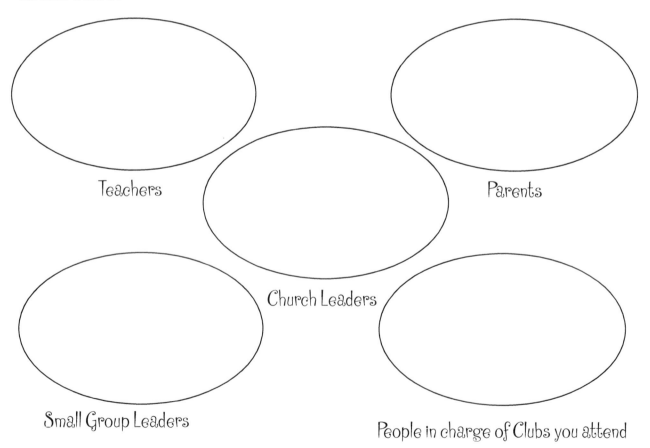

Teachers

Parents

Church Leaders

Small Group Leaders

People in charge of Clubs you attend

Have you ever been in a group when you've been frustrated with the person leading? What's frustrating you? What's bothering you about their leadership? Write out your thoughts.

What are some ways you can honor your leaders, even if you may not love everything about the way they are leading?

What are some ways you can honor the people who are leaders in your life?

Some people who are in authority in your life are your teacher and principals, your parents, policemen, people in governments, and even the President! Cut out some pictures of people in authority and place them here.

The Bible tell us that God gives these people positions of authority. Fill in the blank of our theme verse to show WHO puts people in positions of authority in our lives!

"For all authority comes from _____, and those in positions of authority have been placed there by _____." – Romans 13:1

What are some ways you can respect the people in authority over you?

Activity Sheets

God wants you to be respectful of your elders. It pleases His heart when you honor those in leadership over you.

In the heart draw a picture of you and an elder in your life.

*For all **authority** comes from God, and those in positions of **authority** have been placed there by God.* – Romans 13:1 NLT

What are some ways you can honor the people who are leaders in your life? Unscramble the words to find your answer.

SCRAMBLED WORDS   WRITE YOUR ANSWERS HERE

1. ISELTN   _____

2. OYEB   _____

3. RPAY   _____

4. EAHV A DGOO TDETUTAI   _____

_____

Answers: pray, obey, listen, have a good attitude

Solve the Scripture Puzzle
Step 1: Unscramble each of the clue words to solve the following statement:

An elder is anyone _____ than you, anyone who is in

_____ over you, or anyone who has any kind of

_____ in your life.

CLUE WORDS:

ERDOL ____ ____ ____ ____ ____
       15   14   22   1   17

RILPEAHESD ____ ____ ____ ____ ____ ____ ____ ____ ____ ____
____
       23   2   20   24   6   19   8   12   13   21

TORYUHAIT ____ ____ ____ ____ ____ ____ ____ ____ ____
       18   7   9   16   5   3   10   11   4

Answers: Older, Leadership, Authority

Polka Dot Girls ❀ Relationships

Step 2: Copy the letters in the numbered cells above to the cells below with the same number to discover another scripture regarding authority.

___V___ ___ ___ ___N___   M ___ ___ ___   ___ ___BM ___ ___
1   2   3   4   5   6   7   8   9   8   7   10   11

___ ___M ___ ___ ___F   ___ ___   ___ ___ ___
12   13   8   6   14   9   15   9   16   2

G ___V___ ___N___NG
    5   1   17   10

___ ___ ___ ___ ___ ___ ___ ___ ___ ___ ___,   F___ ___
1   8   7   9   12   5   19   10   9   13   18   5   3

___ ___ ___ ___ ___   ___ ___   N___
9   12   1   17   1   13   8   5

___ ___ ___ ___ ___ ___ ___ ___ ___   ___XC___ ___ ___
20   7   9   16   5   3   13   9   4   1   1   21   11

___ ___ ___ ___   W___ ___C___   G___ ___   ___ ___ ___
9   12   20   9   12   13   12   5   22   12   18   8

___ ___ ___ ___B___ ___ ___ ___ ___ ___   ___ ___ ___
2   8   9   18   23   10   8   12   1   24   11   12   1

___ ___ ___ ___ ___ ___ ___ ___ ___ ___ ___   ___ ___ ___ ___
20   7   9   12   5   19   13   9   13   1   8   9   12   18   11

___X___ ___ ___   ___ ___V___   B___ ___N
2   13   8   9   12   18   1   1   2

___ ___ ___ ___B___ ___ ___ ___ ___ ___   B___   G___ ___.
1   8   11   20   14   13   8   12   1   24   4   5   24

– Romans 13:1 NIV

Weekly Challenge

Grow – Find out who the leaders in your school and community are. Who is the mayor of your town? Who is the principal of your school? Find out their names and then pray for them!

Love – Write a note to say thank you to someone older than you. Tell them that you appreciate all that they bring to your life!

Act – Find a way to help someone older than you this week. Maybe you can open a door for someone, help them clean up their yard, or carry something for them.

Memorize – Memorize the theme verse.

"For all authority comes from God, and those in positions of authority have been placed there by God."

Romans 13:1

Things Change

WHAT'S THE POINT?
EVERYTHING IN THE WORLD CHANGES, BUT GOD WILL NEVER CHANGE.

theme verse
"I am the Lord, and I do not change."
Malachi 3:6

related bible story
The many changes in the life of Joseph
Genesis 39

What is your favorite season? I LOVE the fall. I love it when the leaves are turning different colors. I love it when the weather starts to turn cooler and you pull out your sweaters and boots. I even like it when the stores are filled with back to school supplies. I may not LOVE the idea that my kids are going back to school – but it sure is fun picking out new pencils and erasers and markers, right? Ok… you don't have to answer that question.

Those first days of school are crazy. Talk about changes! Just a few short weeks before school starts, you are at the pool swimming, sleeping in on summer vacation and staying up late playing with your friends. But every year, no matter how much you try and pretend that it isn't coming, the seasons change, summer ends, and fall begins.

THINGS CHANGE.

Another area that it's really easy to see how things change is in the area of fashion. How many of you have seen pictures of your parents from when they were your age or a teenager. Pretty funny, right?

Well, I don't know about you, but I'm pretty glad some things change. I'm glad we don't have to wear some of that stuff!

But you know, not all change is fun. Sometimes change can be really hard. There are a lot of things in my life that have changed and sometimes I've had a really hard time adjusting to those changes.

Change is HARD.

Maybe you have had some things change in your life and you've had a hard time working through them. Maybe you have had to change schools and you are struggling to fit in at your new school and you're really missing your old friends.

Maybe your family has changed. Maybe you have a new brother or sister or maybe things have changed between your parents and you've had to adjust to BIG changes at home.

Maybe your friends are changing. Maybe you have had a friend move away. Or maybe the girls that you used to be really close to just aren't that close any more. Maybe they're starting to be interested in things you aren't interested in and you find yourselves just drifting apart.

Maybe you are dealing with a sickness or something with your health that makes you unable to do things like you used to do, and so you have to change the way you spend your time.

Or maybe YOU are changing. You are getting older. You don't feel the same as you used to and you kind of feel like your whole life is upside down.

Change is hard. And change happens to everyone!

Just when you think you have everything figured out, something happens and you have to start all over again!

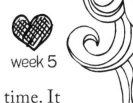

It can be really frustrating to have to deal with things changing all the time. It can make you feel sad, scared, discouraged, and lots of other things. It can make you feel like you are on shaky ground.

How many of you have ever been in a bouncy house? You know, those big things filled with air where you jump up and down. Or maybe you've been on a trampoline with a bunch of other people. Have you ever tried to walk through a bouncy house or walk on a trampoline when other people are jumping all around you?

You try to steady yourself and walk, but with every step the ground around you lifts and dips and moves. You try to shift your weight to keep your balance, but just when you think you have a steady place to stand, the ground beneath you moves again and you fall on your booty!

Sometimes that is EXACTLY how it feels trying to walk through your life when everything around you is changing. You can feel like you can't quite get your footing. You can feel lost. You can feel shaky and insecure. You might be wondering what you can count on when you look at everything around you that keeps changing.

The truth is: things change. Actually, everything in the whole entire world changes and will continue to change except one thing. Do you know what that is?

GOD.

God never changes. He is always the same. Always. Forever. You can count on it.

No matter how many things in your life are changing – He is always the same.

I am the Lord, and I do not change.

Malachi 3:6

God will never, ever change. He is exactly the same today as He has always been. That can be hard for us to understand – because everything around us changes. But the truth is that God will remain EXACTLY the same no matter what.

Hebrews 13:8 says, that "*Jesus Christ is the same yesterday, today, and forever.*" He will NEVER, EVER change.

And so we can lean on God to help us with whatever changes we are going through!

Now imagine that you are back in that bouncy house with everything moving and shaking when suddenly you see a handle along the edge of the wall. You grab onto it and suddenly, even though everything around you is moving, you are able to keep your balance because you are holding onto the handle.

Or imagine that you are on that bouncy-wouncy trampoline. And suddenly a friend who is standing along the edge reaches out a hand to you. As you walk forward, the ground beneath you is still moving like crazy, but you're not falling because you have something steady to hold onto.

You know what? When you are going through changes in your life and you feel like everything is topsy-turvy, GOD will be like that handle that you can grab onto so you can stay steady. When everything around you feels like it's on shaky ground, GOD will be that hand that reaches out and gives you something strong and stable to keep you from falling.

He will be something that you can keep your eyes on while everything else is going crazy around you. He will be someone that will keep you steady when you don't know who or what you can count on! When everything around you is changing, and you don't know what to do, GOD will remain steady and sure.

So, how do we get through all the changes in our lives? What do we do when things around us are changing and we don't know what to do?

⟹ 1. Remember that change is hard.

Polka Dot Girls ❧ Relationships

Can I tell you something? It's ok to be sad about the things that are changing in your world. It's ok to feel upset that your friend doesn't live here anymore. It's ok to be nervous going to a new school or a new church. It's ok to be upset that your parents are having problems. I think it's really important to be honest about how you're feeling.

Have you ever just been in a really BAD mood? You're just cranky and upset and you don't really know why? Sometimes I get that way and the best thing I know to do in those moments is to just sit down and ask myself, "What am I upset about?"

Once I do that, I usually feel a lot better and can start to deal with whatever situation is bothering me instead of just sitting there being a crabby pants.

I think it's important to admit to yourself that you are having a hard time with the changes in your life. And more important than that – it's so good to come to Jesus and tell him about the things that are bothering you. He already knows – cause He knows everything about you! But when we come to Him and pour out our hearts to Him and ask Him to help us deal with the changes in our lives -something really cool happens.

First of all, He will help us! He will give us creative ideas for dealing with the situation. He will give us patience and peace to face anything that comes our way.

And He will also comfort us! This means that when we are feeling sad or upset, God will help us feel better. He will remind you of how much He loves you and just how very special you are to Him. That sure makes me feel better!

The second way that you and I can deal with change in our lives is to

⇒ 2. Remember that God is with you.

There's a story in the Bible about a guy who went through a WHOLE lot of changes. His name was Joseph.

Joseph had twelve brothers. When he was 17 years old, he told his dad some of the bad things that his brothers were doing and after that they did NOT like him at all! So one day, they threw him into a big pit and then they sold him as a slave to Egypt.

Yikes!! Those were some PRETTY big changes for Joseph! His family fell apart and his brothers SOLD him! He had to go to a new country where He didn't know anyone. Can you imagine how hard that would have been?

But God was with Joseph in every change He went through.

Joseph's life was on pretty shaky ground! But no matter what he faced or how crazy things got, God was with Joseph. When he was sad – God was there. When he was scared – God was there. When he was lonely – God was there. When he had no idea what to do – God was there.

And God will be there for you too!

Hebrews 13:5 says, "*Since God assured us, "I'll never let you down, never walk off and leave you.*" (MSG)

When YOU are sad – God will be there.
When YOU are scared – God will be there.
When YOU are lonely – God will be there.
When YOU have no idea what to do – God will be there.

Always. Forever. No exceptions. He is not going anywhere. You can be SURE that He will always be with you – no matter what.

And the last way you deal with change in your life is to:

⇨ 3. Look ahead.

The hardest thing about change is that you MISS the way things were before! You think back to the way things used to be and you can't imagine things being as good as that ever again.

You wonder if you'll ever have as good of friends as you had before. You wonder if you'll ever feel happy with your family with all the new changes. You wonder

if you'll ever like your new school. You wonder if you'll ever feel confident about yourself again.

But – you know what? God has great things AHEAD for you!

You might not be able to see it right now. You might not be able to figure out how it's going to all work out. You might not even feel like it. BUT GOD has great things ahead for you!

1 Peter 1:6 says, "*So be truly glad. There is wonderful joy ahead, even though you have to endure many trials for a little while.*" Things might be hard for a little while when you are dealing with changes, but there is wonderful JOY ahead of you.

The best way to get through a change is to keep your eyes on what is ahead. Philippians 3:13 says, "*Brothers and sisters, I myself don't think I've reached it, but I do this one thing: I forget about the things behind me and reach out for the things ahead of me.*" (CEB)

Now, to forget what is behind – does that mean that we can't still love our old friends? Does it mean we can't remember how great those old times were? Does it mean you can't wish your family would be the way it used to be?

No Way! What is DOES mean is that you can't stop living your life and get STUCK where you are because you won't look ahead to what God has for you. You can remember and love ALL the things that used to be – and still reach out for all the things that God has planned for your future.

God has GREAT things ahead of you! He has new friends for you to meet. He has new things He wants you to do. He has plans to help you deal with your new family situation.

He has new things for you to learn. He has new places for you to make a difference. And great big exciting things for every area of your life.

And HE is going to BE THERE for each and every one of them.

James 1:17 says, "*Every good gift, every perfect gift, comes from above. These gifts come down from* the Father, the Creator of the heavenly lights, in whose character there is no change at all." (CEB)

You can look forward to what God has for you because you KNOW that He is going to be there. Hebrews 1:10-11 says, "*Earth and sky will wear out, but not you; they become threadbare like an old coat; You'll fold them up like a worn-out cloak, and lay them away on the shelf. But you'll stay the same, year after year; you'll never fade, you'll never wear out.*" (MSG)

Everything changes. People change. Circumstances change. Families change. Jobs and schools change.

BUT GOD NEVER, EVER CHANGES.

Closing Prayer: *Dear God, There are a lot of things that are changing in my life. I need you to help me work through these things in my life. Help me to know that you are with me, and to trust that you have great things in store for my future. I love you. Amen.*

My
Polka Dot
SPOT

week 5

Everything in the world changes. Maybe *YOU* have had some things in your family, your school, or your friends that are not the same as they used to be. Write out some things that have changed in your life right here.

How do you feel about these changes? On your list above, draw a happy face next to the changes that you are happy about and draw a sad face next to the changes that have been hard for you.

When everything in our lives feels shaky or unsteady (like walking in a bouncy house or on a trampoline) God will be the steady hand we can hold onto because He *Never* changes. Draw a picture of God holding your hand in the space below.

Our theme verse for this week is Malachi 3:6, "*I am the Lord, and I do not change.*" Decorate the area around the verse with stickers, ribbon, glitter, or any other pretty thing. As you make the page your very own... practice saying the verse until you have it memorized!

"I am the Lord, and I do not change."

- Malachi 3:6

It's important to remember that no matter what changes are going on in your life, God will always be with you. How does that make you feel when you know that God will never leave your side?

Maybe you're having a hard time looking ahead and you need God to help you look forward. Ask God to help you see what lies ahead. Write out some of the new things that you think God has planned for you. List some ideas here or draw some pictures of the things you have to look forward to!

God is our Rock Booklet

Instructions:

- Tear out the cover and the four seasons worksheets
- Color and decorate the cover and each page according to the season.
- Draw a picture of yourself and your family or friends doing your favorite activity in each season!
- Staple the cover and the four pages to make a booklet

Seasons Change, but GOD does NOT!

By: _____

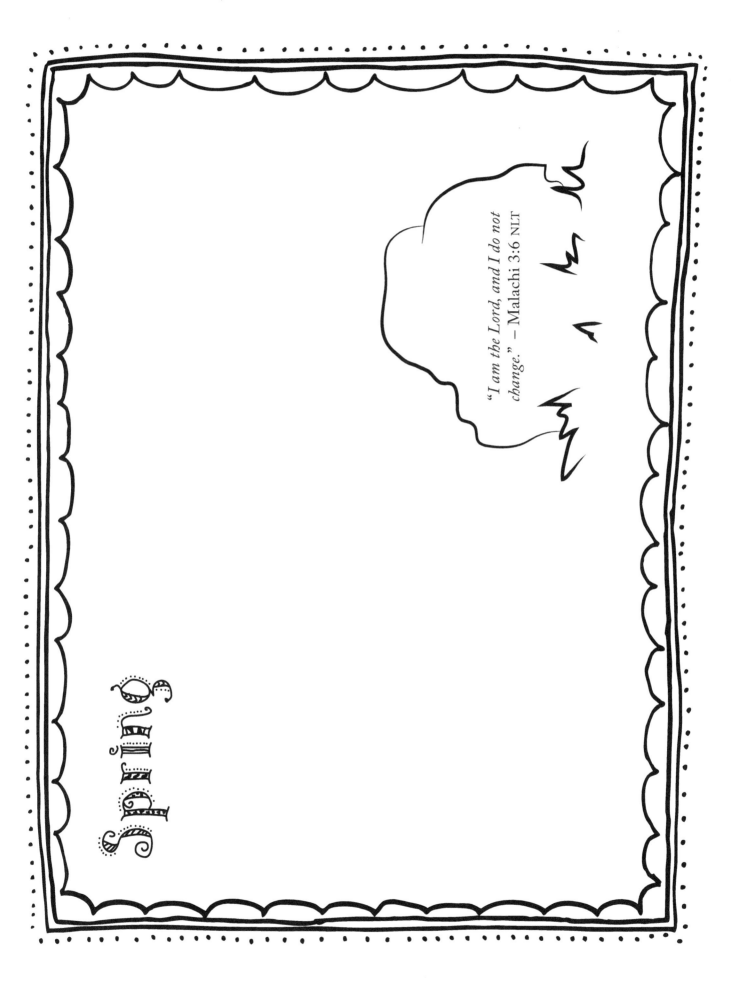

Spring

"I am the Lord, and I do not change." – Malachi 3:6 NLT

Fall

"I am the Lord, and I do not change." – Malachi 3:6 NLT

"I am the Lord, and I do not change." – Malachi 3:6 NLT

Winter

Summer

"I am the Lord, and I do not change." – Malachi 3:6 NLT

Activity Sheets

Instructions: Finish the rest of the butterfly with your best doodles, then color the caterpillar and butterfly!

I CHANGE, BUT GOD DOES NOT!

List 5 things that have changed in your life over the last year.

1.

2.

3.

4.

5.

List 5 new things God has ahead for you.

1.

2.

3.

4.

5.

Look up the following verses in your Bible and fill in the blanks. All scripture NIV

"I the LORD do not _____*."* – Malachi 3:6

"Jesus Christ is the _____ *yesterday and today and forever."*

– Hebrews 13:8

"But you remain the _____, *and your years will never end."*

– Psalm 102:27

"Every good and perfect gift is from above, coming down from the Father of the heavenly lights, who does not _____ *like shifting shadows."*

– James 1:17

"Brothers, I do not consider myself yet to have taken hold of it. But one thing I do: Forgetting what is _____ *and straining toward what is* _____*,"* – Philippians 3:13

"In this you greatly _____*, though now for a little while you may have had to suffer grief in all kinds of trials."* – 1 Peter 1:6

"Keep your lives free from the love of money and be _____ *with what you have, because God has said, "Never will I* _____ *you; never will I* _____ *you."* – Hebrews 13:5

WORD LIST

change	*rejoice*	*content*	*same*
leave	*change*	*forsake*	*behind*
same	*ahead*		

Weekly Challenge

Grow – Grow closer to God as you talk to Him about how you feel about the changes in your life.

Love – Maybe you have a friend who has had a big change happen in her life. Do something special to remind her that God is with her. Write her a note, draw her a picture, or maybe just give her a hug!

Act – Make a list of some of the things that have changed in your life. Then, make a list of some of the new things that God has in front of you.

Memorize – Memorize the theme verse.

"I am the Lord, and I do not change."
Malachi 3:6

Watch Your Words

WHAT'S THE POINT?

GOD WANTS US TO CHOOSE TO USE KIND AND ENCOURAGING WORDS.

theme verse

"Words kill, words give life;
they're either poison or fruit—you choose."
Proverbs 18:21 MSG

related bible story

Taming the Tongue

James 3:5-12

Have you ever had someone say something really, really nice about you? Maybe your Mom told everyone in your family something really special about you. Or maybe a teacher pointed out how much she appreciated your help in class. Or maybe a friend thanked you for being in her life.

There is nothing quite as awesome as someone saying something nice to you. Something inside of you just feels SO good when someone speaks kind words to you. You feel happy, confident and proud of yourself. I love it when people say nice things about me!!!

Now, let me ask you THIS question. Have you ever had someone say something "not so nice" about you? Yup… me too. Maybe a friend got mad at you and said some things about you behind your back. Or maybe a teacher said something that hurt your feelings. Or maybe your brother or sister called you a name.

103

There is nothing quite as AWFUL as having someone say something bad about you. You get a horrible feeling in your stomach and you just want to crawl into bed and cry. You feel sad, nervous, and alone. I HATE it when people say bad things about me!

Isn't it crazy to see how POWERFUL our words are? A kind word from someone can make you feel AMAZING and an unkind word can make you feel HORRIBLE. I think it is amazing how something as little as a WORD can have so much power over how we feel.

The Bible says that *"Words kill, words give life; they're either poison or fruit—you choose."* (Proverbs 18:21 MSG) What do you think that means? It means that our words have the power to tear people down or build people up. And you and I have to choose what kind of words we are going to use.

Sarah hated going to the bus stop. Every morning she would get on her coat and shoes and backpack and head for the front door and stop and say a prayer because she was SO nervous to walk outside to wait for the bus with the other kids.

The reason WHY she was so nervous was because there were three girls at the bus stop who didn't say very nice things to her. Every morning, they would comment on what she was wearing and whisper and giggle at her. Sarah had NO idea why these girls were so mean to her, but it seemed like no matter what she did, they found something bad to say about her.

Their words were powerful. Even if Sarah got dressed and looked at her outfit and absolutely LOVED it, once the girls at the bus stop finished with her, she always felt horrible about what she was wearing. Their words hurt.

The Bible tells us that our words have the power to hurt, but they also have the power to build someone up. Our words can tear down, but our words also have the power to make us feel stronger and more confident!

One day Sarah got to the bus stop and was bracing herself for the girls to start talking about her. But before they could open their mouths, suddenly another girl spoke up. "Sarah, I love your new

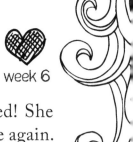

coat! I think it is really cool. Where did you get it?" Sarah was shocked! She replied quietly, "Uhm... my Grandma sent it to me." The other girl spoke again. "Well, I think it is the cutest thing I've ever seen... but you always wear the cutest clothes."

Sarah could not believe it. She looked at the mean girls and their mouths were wide open and they simply turned away in a huff. The nice things that this girl said to her quieted the rude comments of the other girls. The power of those nice words was WAY stronger than the power of the negative ones. She was so thankful that this new friend has chosen to use the power of kind words instead of the power of unkind words.

I know that sometimes it can be hard to control the words that are coming from your mouth. There are times that I say things and then I wonder "Why in the world did I say that?!?" It can be easy to say mean things to someone when you are frustrated with them. It can make you feel strong when you use the power of your words to tear someone else down. And you can feel important when you talk about another person.

But God is very clear in the Bible that He wants us to be very, very careful about the words we use. James 3:2 says, "*For if we could control our tongues, we would be perfect and could also control ourselves in every other way.*" God knows that if we control our tongues – or if we control the things we say - that we will be able to control ourselves in lots of different areas. Our words may be hard to control, but if we learn to be careful about the things we are saying, we will be able to control LOTS of other things in our hearts!

Here are three ways we can choose to use the power of our words for GOOD and not EVIL.

⇒ 1. Don't gossip.

Gossip is simply talking about other people behind their backs. It is sharing information or stories with other people. Most of the time, it's sharing things that are mean and hurtful, but it's even wrong to simply share information that isn't yours to share! Gossip is telling a story that can damage a person's reputation. It is talking or writing about another person or situation in order to turn another's opinion against that person or situation.

Sometimes we gossip because we are upset with a person and we don't know what to do about it. But the Bible tells us that if we have a problem with someone, we shouldn't talk to other people about it – we should go right to the person and talk it through with them! Matthew 18:15 says, "*If a fellow believer hurts you, GO and tell him – work it out between the two of you.*"

Other times we gossip just because it seems fun. Sometimes we can talk about other people simply because we don't have anything better to talk about. Some people just think it's fun to say things about people's clothes or families or lots of other things. We can tell our friends a story that we may think is funny, but really we are just making fun of someone else.

But God does **NOT** want us to use other people that way. He cares about each and every person and when we say things about other people, it makes God's heart so sad. We should want to honor God by treating other people the way that God would want us to treat them. Psalm 19:14 says, "*Let the words of my mouth and the thoughts of my heart be pleasing to you O Lord.*"

God wants you to be a good friend. When we talk about other people behind their backs, we are not being a good friend.

Another way we can choose positive words is

➡ 2. **Be a trustworthy friend.**

I had a friend who liked to talk about other people. She loved to tell what so-and-so did last weekend and who is fighting with whom. She loved to go through all the people we knew and point out all the things about them that she didn't like. She just **LOVED** to talk about other people.

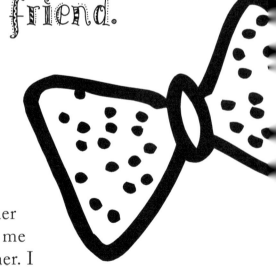

I never felt comfortable when she talked about other people that way. But one day, something occurred to me that made me really re-think my friendship with her. I began to wonder – if she talked about OTHER PEOPLE all the time behind their backs, chances are she was talking about ME behind my back.

But I have ANOTHER friend, who NEVER talks about other people. And anytime we are with other people and they start to say something about someone else, she either says something positive about that person or changes the subject. I really began to notice how hard she worked at not saying unkind things about people.

That friend made me realize two things. First of all, that I should be a lot more like her!! And secondly, I realized that I could always trust her. I never had to wonder if she was saying bad things about me to other people. I could tell her anything and know that she wouldn't share it with anyone else.

I realized that the way this friend acted made me TRUST her. When you trust someone, it means that you feel safe with them. You don't wonder if they are REALLY your friend or not. You don't have to worry about them behaving one way when they are with you and another way when you're not around.

Not only should you try to fill your life with friends you can trust, you should BECOME a trustworthy friend! Make sure your friends know that they can count on you to only use kind words about them. Show them your loyalty by refusing to talk about ANYONE behind their back. Proverbs 20:19 says, *"A gossip tells secrets, so don't hang around with someone who talks too much."*

The last way we can be a friend who chooses positive words, is to

3. **Encourage other people.**

We have talked about how powerful our words are. They can build people up, or they can tear them down. We can choose to use kind words or we can choose to use unkind words.

When you say kind words to people, you are encouraging them! When you point out the good things in people, and tell them what you like about them, you are encouraging them! When you help people feel better about themselves, you are an encourager!

Imagine that each one of us has a bucket. We'll call it our LOVE bucket. When someone says something kind and encouraging to you, they are filling up your love bucket. When more encouraging things that are said to you, your bucket gets fuller and fuller and you feel more loved and confident!

But when someone says something unkind to you, they are emptying your love bucket. Each negative word, harsh comment, and moment of gossip takes all the love out of our love bucket and eventually we can find our bucket totally empty.

Now, I don't know about you, but I want to be the kind of friend who is always filling up the love buckets of the people in my life. I never want to be emptying out their bucket! I want to make sure that I am saying encouraging things, using kind words, and being a positive person so that I am constantly filling up the love buckets of my friends and family!

Ephesians 4:29 tell us, "*Let everything you say be good and helpful, so that your words will be an encouragement to those who hear them.*" Make a decision to be the kind of friend who always says good and helpful things. Be an encouraging friend.

Our words are powerful. We can choose to use our words to encourage and lift up our friends, or we can choose to use our words to tear them down. Let's be the kind of friends who make the right choice!

Closing Prayer: *Dear God, I thank you for the friends and family you have given me. Help me to not use words that tear down other people. Help me to not talk about people behind their backs. I want to be a trustworthy and encouraging friend. I love you, Jesus. Amen.*

My Polka Dot SPOT

Have you ever had someone say something really nice to you? Write out your experience here.

How did it make you feel when that person said something kind to you?

Has someone ever said something unkind to you? How did that make you feel?

109

The Bible tells us that our words are powerful, and we have a choice as to whether we are going to use kind or unkind words. Our theme verse is "*Words kill, words give life; they're either poison or fruit—you choose.*" – Proverbs 18:21 MSG

Below you will find a picture of a bottle of poison and a piece of fruit. In the bottle picture, write out some things that you could say to your friends that would be like poison to them. In the picture of the fruit, write out some things you could say to your friends that would be life giving and make them feel better about themselves.

What does it mean to gossip?

What does God say about gossip?

What are some ways you can be a trustworthy friend?

God wants you to be an encouraging friend and to fill up your friends' love buckets. Glue a picture of one of your friends onto the picture of the bucket (or write her name if you don't have a picture.)

In, or around the hearts, write some encouraging things that you think about your friend. When you're done, you can tear out this page and give it to your friend!

Encouraging Word Notepad

Make this fun notepad for your desk or locker to write quick notes of encouragement to your friends!

Supplies Needed:
- Scrap Cardboard
- 3" square self-stick notepad
- Construction Paper or Scrapbook Paper
- Scissors and/or Decorative Edging Scissors
- Stickers or pretty embellishments
- Glue Stick
- Hot Glue Gun
- Ribbon (optional)
- Magnet (optional)

What Should I Do Next?
- Cut the scrap cardboard into a 5 ½" square.
- Cut construction or decorative paper to fit on top of the square.
- Glue the paper on top of the cardboard with a glue stick.
- Attach the self-stick notepad with a hot glue gun in the center of the covered cardboard.
- Decorate the covered cardboard edges with stickers and/or pretty embellishments.
- Attach ribbon at the back of the covered cardboard to hang. (optional)
- Attach a magnet at the back of the covered cardboard to hang. (optional)
- Write notes of encouragement!

Activity Sheets

Each word or phrase has the power to encourage others or hurt others.

Color the encouraging words and draw a line through the words that hurt.

"Words kill, words give life; they're either poison or fruit—you choose."
– Proverbs 18:21 MSG

WAY TO GO!

YOU ARE AWESOME

I DON'T LIKE YOU

I LOVE YOU

YOU CAN DO IT!

THAT'S STUPID

I BELIEVE IN YOU

YOU CAN'T PLAY WITH ME

THANK YOU FOR BEING MY FRIEND

YOU ARE SO GOOD AT THAT!

YOU ARE SO MEAN

I DON'T CARE WHAT YOU SAY

YOU DON'T FIT IN OUR GROUP

God is very clear in the Bible that He wants us to be very, very careful about the words we use. Your words can build up those around you or tear them down.

Fill in the blanks below to start building up the friends and family in your life.

I can build up _____ with this word of encouragement:

I can build up _____ with this compliment:

I can build up _____ by thanking them for:

I can build up _____ by telling them this about God:

God wants us to choose to use kind and encouraging words.

The verses below talk about how we should watch our words. Read each verse in your Bible and fill in the missing word. All scripture NIV

1. James 3:2

"We all stumble in many ways. If anyone is never at fault in what he says, he is a perfect man, able to keep his whole _____ in check."

2. Psalm 19:14

"May the words of my mouth and the meditation of my _____ be pleasing in your sight, O LORD, my Rock and my Redeemer."

3. Ephesians 4:29

"Do not let any unwholesome talk come out of your _____, but only what is helpful for building others up according to their needs, that it may benefit those who _____."

4. Proverbs 20:19

"A _____ betrays a confidence; so avoid a man who talks too much."

5. Matthew 18:15

"If your brother _____ against you, go and show him his fault, just between the _____ of you. If he listens to you, you have won your brother over."

WORD LIST

heart	two	body	listen
gossip	sins	mouths	

119

Weekly Challenge

Grow – Grow by reading James 3:5-12 which talks about controlling the things we say!

Love – Show love to your friends by being a trustworthy friend. When other people start sharing gossip, change the subject or say something nice about that person instead. You will prove that you can be a friend who can be trusted!

Act – Think of some encouraging things you can say to fill up your friends' love buckets and then **TELL** them!

Memorize – Memorize the theme verse:

"Words kill, words give life; they're either poison or fruit—you choose."

Proverbs 18:21 MSG

Attention

WHAT'S THE POINT?

WE SHOULD BE KNOWN FOR THE GOOD THINGS WE DO — AND NOT TRY TO GET ATTENTION FROM THE THINGS WE WEAR, TRYING TO BE THE CENTER OF ATTENTION, OR DOING NEGATIVE THINGS.

theme verse

For women who claim to be devoted to God should make themselves attractive by the good things they do.

I Timothy 2:10

related bible story

Tabitha

Acts 9:36-43

I L-O-V-E birthdays.

I love everything about them. I love all the presents. I love the cake and candles. But mostly, it sure is fun to have a day where everyone points out how special you are. It's so nice to have people say nice things to you and give you gifts. It's fun to have a day where you are the center of attention.

Can you imagine if everyday was your birthday?! If everywhere you went, everyday, people stopped you and handed you a gift! Or after every meal, your mom brought out a cake and everyone sang to you?! That would be crazy.... *Crazy awesome!*

Birthdays are fun because it's always nice to get attention. It feels good when people notice you and tell you that you are special to them. Really, I think for most of us, one of the things most important to us is to feel like we matter to the people around us. We want to know that people love us and care about us. And on our birthdays, people take extra time to make sure we KNOW how important we are to them. It's really, really, nice!

But, what about all those other days? There are 364 days every year that are NOT your birthday. What do we do on those days when we aren't getting special attention? Some of you don't really like attention, so you are just fine on the non-birthday days! But for most of us, sometimes we can need more attention than we are getting from those plain everyday days.

Why does attention feel so good? Because we all want to know that we are valuable. We want to know that we are important to people. We want to feel loved and pretty and liked. When someone gives you attention by saying something nice to you, it makes your heart happy and you feel good about yourself. When someone gives you attention by asking you to spend time with them, you feel important. When someone tells you that you are beautiful, you feel beautiful!

There is nothing wrong with getting attention from other people. Actually, God loves it when we feel good about ourselves because He LOVES us. HE is your #1 fan. He loves every single tiny thing about you. So, when other people value you, He likes it too!

But sometimes, we can get the WRONG kind of attention. People can notice us because of the negative things we do. We can behave in a way that isn't kind and loving and other people notice us for the wrong reason.

There was a girl in Kathy's class that always seemed to have the teacher's attention, but Kathy wasn't so sure that it was the "good kind" of attention. This girl was always getting in trouble for being disrespectful. She would be speak out of turn and say inappropriate things. The teacher spent a lot of time dealing with this girl's behavior. She sure was getting a lot of attention, but it wasn't for positive things.

And sometimes we can get attention by doing or saying things that aren't very honoring to God. Sometimes we can wear clothes that are a little too sassy and people can notice us in a "not so good" kind of way. God doesn't like it when we get that kind of attention. Sometimes we can get attention by telling a joke that has a bad word in it or saying mean things about other people. God doesn't want us to get attention like that either.

Here are three things to remember when it comes to attention.

⇒ 1. Don't steal all the attention.

Candace had a friend that REALLY loved to get attention. She loved to talk about the things SHE was doing and point out the new outfit SHE was wearing and make sure everyone knew what SHE wanted to do. She was super nice and really fun to be around, but it seemed like she always had to be the center of attention. After a while, her friends got tired of everything ALWAYS being about her. They got frustrated because she never seemed interested in listening to what THEY had to say. If the conversation wasn't focused on the things that she wanted to talk about, then she simply would stop listening.

God doesn't want us stealing all the attention! He doesn't want us to always make things about ourselves. ACTUALLY, the Bible says, "*Don't be selfish; don't try to impress others. Be humble, thinking of others as better than yourselves.*" – Philippians 2:3. When we are constantly demanding all the attention, we are really being selfish. We are not thinking of other people's feelings; we are simply focusing on ourselves and what we want.

Good friends are interested in what other people have to say. Good friends love to point out the wonderful things in other people. Good friends don't steal all the attention.

Secondly, we need to remember:

➡ 2. Don't try to get attention in negative ways.

It certainly is nice to have people pay attention to you, but sometimes we can start to want it so bad that we're willing to do anything to make people notice us. One way we can do that is by misbehaving just to get someone's attention. We can act out in school, disobey our parents at home, and even fight with our friends. We may be getting attention all right, but it's not for good things!

And sometimes we can try and get attention by doing or saying things that we know we shouldn't say or do. We can put on clothes that make people notice us, but they make us look a way that isn't pleasing to God. The Bible talks about not drawing attention to ourselves by wearing things that make people notice us in a negative way. I Timothy 2:9 says, *"And I want women to be modest in their appearance. They should wear decent and appropriate clothing and not draw attention to themselves by the way they fix their hair or by wearing gold or pearls or expensive clothes."* Now, does this mean that you can't wear cute clothes or fun jewelry?! NO!

What this scripture is saying is that we need to dress in clothes that cover up our bodies in a way that doesn't look too sassy. Sometimes we can see clothes that are really, really short or have things about them that seem really grown up. We want to make sure that the clothes we wear don't draw SO much attention to us that people only notice what we are wearing, and not what's on the inside!

Don't try to get attention from things that aren't good. You are such an amazing and beautiful girl; you don't need all that stuff to make people notice you! You just be the bright shining light that God made you to be – and people will notice you for that!

And the last thing we need to remember is:

➡ 3. Be known for the good things you do for other people.

Polka Dot Girls ❀ Relationships

There is a story in the Bible about a woman who was known for all the amazing, kind, and generous things she did. Her name was Tabitha. (She is also called Dorcus sometimes. I'm not sure I would like to be called Dorcus... would you?!?) Acts 9:36 says, "*There was a believer in Joppa named Tabitha (which in Greek is Dorcas). She was always doing kind things for others and helping the poor.*" One day she became very sick and died. A man named Peter, who was one of Jesus' disciples, was called to the house where she lived.

"*So Peter returned with them; and as soon as he arrived, they took him to the upstairs room. The room was filled with widows who were weeping and showing him the coats and other clothes Dorcas had made for them.*" (Acts 9:39) The house was full of people who knew and loved Tabitha because of the kind things she had done for them. It says that she had made them coats and sewed clothes for them. These were women whose husband's had died and were probably very, very poor. Tabitha had taken it upon herself to take care of them, and that was what she was known for! (PS... you should read the rest of the story in Acts Chapter 9... because something totally crazy incredible happens to Tabitha!!!)

POLKA DOT POINTERS

The name Tabitha is a Hebrew name. Other times in the Bible, they call her by the name Dorcas, which is a Greek name. Both of the words mean "gazelle" which is kind of like a deer. The Bible was originally written in these two languages, the Old Testament in Hebrew, and the New Testament in Greek! I am thankful for the people who translated the Bible into English from these two languages so that I can read it and understand it!!

125

What I LOVE about this story is the fact that for all the other things that Tabitha could have been known for, she was known as the woman who cared for other people. People loved her because she truly helped other people. She wasn't always thinking about herself and how she could get attention for herself. NO! She thought of others first and how she could help them. That is the kind of attention I want!

We all love to get attention. But God wants us to be confident in Him, and not need to get so much attention from other people. When we know that God loves us, and that He thinks we are the most amazing girl in the world, we don't need to grab all the attention we can get from other people. We can feel strong and beautiful because we KNOW on the inside that we are important and matter to God.

Closing Prayer: *Dear God. I pray that you help me to care for other people and not try and get attention in ways that aren't pleasing to you. Help me to be known for good things. I thank you that you love me and think I'm amazing! Amen.*

Aren't birthday's fun! Print out some pictures of your favorite birthday moments and glue them here OR draw a picture of you celebrating your birthday!

Why is it so much fun to have birthdays?

God doesn't want us to steal all the attention. What are some ways in which we can try and get all the attention focused on us?

Think of some times when either you or someone you know has tried to steal all the attention. What did they do? And how did that make you feel?

One of the verse we read today said that "*women should dress modestly...*" To dress 𝕄𝕆𝔻𝔼𝕊𝕋𝕃𝕐 means to wear clothes that aren't too sassy. We shouldn't wear clothes that look too grown up and make people look at us in a negative way. And we want to make sure our shorts and skirts aren't too short and that our shirts cover up our chest. Go through some magazines and cut out pictures of girls who are dressed 𝕄𝕆𝔻𝔼𝕊𝕋𝕃𝕐 and glue them here.

Tabitha was known for the good things she did and how she took care of other people. What are some good things YOU are known for?

"Do Good" Helping Hand Cookies

Make these awesome cookies with a parent, and make sure you give them away to someone special!

Ingredients:

For Dough
- 2 cups sifted all-purpose flour, plus more for dusting

- 1/4 teaspoon table salt

- 1/2 teaspoon baking powder

- 8 tablespoons (1 stick) unsalted butter

- 1 cup sugar

- 1 large egg

- 1 teaspoon pure vanilla extract, for decorating

For Decorating
- 1 large egg white

- 1 teaspoon water

- Sanding sugar

Directions:
- In a large bowl, sift together flour, salt, and baking powder. Set aside.

- With an electric mixer, beat together the butter and sugar on medium speed until fluffy, about 3 minutes. Add egg, and beat until smooth, about 1 minute.

- Add reserved flour mixture, and mix on low speed until thoroughly combined. Stir in vanilla. Wrap dough in plastic, and refrigerate for about 45 minutes.

- Make cookie pattern while wrapped dough is chilling. For the pattern, trace your hand on a manila file folder, and cut out the tracing. You will lay this on the dough and trace around it with the tip of a paring knife.

- Preheat oven to 325 degrees. Line 2 baking sheets with parchment paper. On a well-floured work surface, roll out cold dough to 1/8 inch thick. Cut out hand shapes. Transfer cookies to prepared baking sheets. Refrigerate until firm, about 15 minutes. Dough scraps may be re-rolled twice.

- Bake until edges just begin to brown lightly, 8 to 10 minutes. Let cookies cool on pans for 3 minutes before transferring to wire racks to cool completely.

- Decorate the cookies with your favorite icing and decorations.

Activity Sheets

Tabitha was known as the woman who cared for other people. People loved her because she truly helped them. She wasn't always thinking about herself and how she could get attention for herself.

Draw a picture of yourself helping someone!

Like Tabitha, God wants us to think of others above ourselves.

Fill in the missing letters in the verse below by substituting each number with the letter in the key to discover God's message.

For w___men who claim to be ___evoted to ___ ___ ___
         2   3   1   2   3

should make themselves attractive by the ___ ___ ___ ___ things
                                       1   2   2   3

they ___ ___. – 1 Timothy 2:10 NLT
       3   2

KEY

G O D
1 2 3

Read the amazing story of Tabitha in Acts 9:36-43 in your NIV Bible.

Step 1: Fill in the missing words.

"In Joppa there was a disciple named _____ (which, when translated, is _____), who was always doing _____ and _____ the poor. About that time she became sick and died, and her body was washed and placed in an _____ room.

_____ was near Joppa; so when the disciples heard that _____ was in Lydda, they sent two men to him and urged him, "Please come at once!"

Peter went with them, and when he arrived he was taken upstairs to the room. All the _____ stood around him, crying and showing him the _____ and other clothing that Dorcas had _____ while she was still with them.

Polka Dot Girls ❧ Relationships

Peter sent them all out of the room; then he got down on his knees and _____. Turning toward the dead woman, he said, "Tabitha, get up." She _____ her eyes, and seeing Peter she sat up. He took her by the _____ and helped her to her feet. Then he called the _____ and the widows and presented her to them _____. This became known all over Joppa, and many people believed in the _____. Peter stayed in Joppa for some time with a tanner named Simon."

Step 2: Find the missing words in the Word Search puzzle.

WORD SEARCH PUZZLE

```
Z  V  R  S  R  D  R  O  B  E  S  L  A  F  O  P
O  F  K  O  P  E  Y  O  R  W  Y  A  N  S  D  E
X  T  L  D  E  N  E  P  O  D  T  F  F  Z  E  C
T  C  D  M  M  E  Z  D  D  G  N  N  L  T  E  E
E  G  O  Q  S  R  I  A  T  S  P  U  T  A  M  R
C  O  R  D  R  W  H  H  R  G  N  I  B  F  E  O
D  E  C  J  L  T  P  E  T  E  R  C  Z  E  Z  E
R  H  U  T  I  E  V  L  A  S  F  K  V  O  S  W
C  L  S  B  R  E  F  P  D  H  D  I  S  K  M  I
D  N  A  H  I  L  S  I  R  O  L  Y  B  X  X  T
S  T  K  L  R  K  O  N  O  A  E  D  A  M  G  O
O  T  E  V  O  S  F  G  L  J  Y  Z  T  R  G  Z
I  B  S  P  M  K  E  N  X  D  J  E  L  O  D  L
H  O  M  E  T  H  E  Z  R  F  O  I  D  R  S  E
K  Y  E  N  N  I  C  E  G  I  E  Z  S  T  O  G
U  A  J  P  X  H  O  S  E  R  S  C  Z  C  A  E
```

WORD LIST

Tabitha	*good*	*helping*	*upstairs*	*alive*
widows	*believers*	*robes*	*made*	*opened*
hand	*prayed*	*Lydda*	*Lord*	*Dorcus*
Peter				

Weekly Challenge

Grow – Grow your faith by reading the story of Tabitha in Acts 9:32-43

Love – Show your love for your friends by not stealing all the attention. Ask them what they want to do or listen to what they have to say!

Act – Tabitha was known for the kind things she did for others. Think of something kind you can do for a someone this week and DO IT!

Memorize – Memorize 1 Timothy 2:10

"For women who claim to be devoted to God should make themselves attractive by the good things they do."

Mean Girls

WHAT'S THE POINT?

DON'T BE A MEAN GIRL. AND LOVE THE MEAN GIRLS IN YOUR LIFE.

theme verse

"Love your enemies! Do good to those who hate you.
Bless those who curse you. Pray for those who hurt you."
Luke 6:27-28

related bible story

King David
Psalm 55

Sometimes girls are mean.

And it really stinks.

Remember we talked earlier about God's super secret weapon in how to deal with relationships? What was the verse? *"Treat people in the same way that you want them to treat you."* – Luke 6:31 CEB

So – wouldn't it just be the most amazing thing in the world if everyone else treated YOU the way that they wanted to be treated?! If they only spoke kind words to you and never picked on you and never got mad at you? I think that would be ah-mazing.

But unfortunately, that's not the way things are. Even if you are kind and loving, there will be moments when other people say mean things, treat you poorly, and generally make life stink.

Alannah had so much fun playing with the girls on her street... most of the time. Some days they could have the best time EVER, and then the next day the girls would get mad at her and leave her house angry and say all kinds of mean things to her. She never really knew what to expect when she was going out to spend time with those girls.

And the WORST part was that she was starting to see herself behaving in the same way. She got tired of always being the one yelled at, so she started yelling back. It seemed like the only way to get them to listen to her was if she did the same things to them that they were doing to her. But in her heart she knew that this wasn't the way that good friends treated one another.

So – what should Alannah do? And what should you and I do when we're in a situation where it seems like there is LOTS of drama and fighting and maybe even someone picking on us for no reason? What does God want us to do?

Well, thankfully, God gives us some answers in the Bible to help us deal with all of these situations. I'm not saying that it will be easy... but doing the right thing is very rarely easy.

First of all,

⇒ 1. Don't Do Drama!

We have a saying at our house whenever anyone is going to play with friends. We say, "Don't Do Drama!" Now what in the world does that mean? Well, when you're with your friends, sometimes things can get tense pretty quick. Just like what Alannah was having with her friends! One friend gets mad at the other friend because the other friend didn't do what the one friend wanted to do and so the first friend storms out of the house saying, "I'm not going to be your friend anymore" and the other friend yells back, "Well, you're not coming to my birthday party then" and then the other friend starts crying and runs to tell

Polka Dot Girls ❀ Relationships

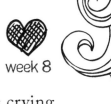

her Mom that her friend is being mean and then the other friend starts crying because she's afraid she's going to get in trouble when it was really the other friend who started it all………and it goes on and on and on. You know what all THAT is called? Drama! When you get upset easily… it's drama. When you make a huge scene over a little thing… it's drama. When you say mean things to your friend… it's drama.

So, instead of having these crazy fights with your friends all the time, what if you decided to just "Don't Do Drama?!" What that means is that instead of getting emotional and reacting in such a BIG way when your friend does something you don't like, you just calmly talk it out. When your friend says something that upsets you, instead of coming back at her with something just as sassy, what if you just said, "I'm sorry you feel that way, how can we work this out?"

Proverbs 29:11 says, "*A foolish person lets his anger run wild. But a wise person keeps himself under control.*" (NIRV) You can get angry and frustrated, but learn to talk about things with your friends and work them out calmly without all the drama. Cause you know what, the drama just makes everything worse.

SO – next time you are having a disagreement with your friend, and you are tempted to start getting emotional and angry, say to yourself "Don't Do Drama" and find a calm way to talk through your issues.

(Oh yeah… and if your friend continues to "DO DRAMA" even when you're trying not to, don't give up. Just ignore it and move onto something else. It's takes two people to have a fight and if you simply don't dive into the mess, she will eventually calm down too!!)

The second thing we need to remember when dealing with mean people is,

2. Love your enemies.

Casey was picked on by a girl at school ALL THE TIME. She made fun of her clothes. She made fun of her school work. She made fun of her family. She talked about her to other people. She made Casey's life MISERABLE.

She didn't know what to do. She talked to her Mom about it, and they met with her teacher and the other girl and her parents. She was really embarrassed, but she knew that it was important to tell a grown up what was going on.

After the meeting, things got better, but something in Casey's heart got worse. She was SO angry at this girl. How could someone treat another person that way? Why did she do those things? Inside, she just wanted to get back at her. But she knew that God wanted her to forgive the person who had hurt her. She knew that the Bible said, "*Love your enemies! Do good to those who hate you. Bless those who curse you. Pray for those who hurt you.*" (Luke 6:27-28)

So, she asked God to help her love her enemy. She began to pray for the person who had hurt her so badly.
She showed kindness to her, even though she really wanted to punch her in the face! And she didn't say bad things about her to other people.

Something amazing happened when Casey decided to do what the Bible said. Her heart began to feel better. She didn't feel as angry any more. Actually, God softened her heart so that she could see that this girl was really just scared and insecure.

Now, it's not like she suddenly wanted to be her best friend! And she didn't start hanging out with her or anything like that. She didn't even really LIKE her. But God helped her love her by seeing her as one of God's daughters… just like she was. She knew that God loved this girl – and so she could love her and pray that she would get to know Jesus and that He would change her heart.

God will help you love your enemies.

But, what about another group of people? What about people who USED to be your friends and now they won't be your friend anymore?

⇨ 3. Ask God to help you with broken relationships.

It's one thing to have a stranger pick on you and be mean to you… but it's a whole other thing when someone who USED to be a close friend suddenly won't be your friend anymore and is mean to you. I think this is one of the most painful things we can experience in our relationships. It is REALLY hard when our relationships are broken and someone who used to be our friend is now the person who is hurting us.

I think it hurts so much because they know so much about you! They were close to you and know what you're really like. It can be really hard because you can feel like you're not good enough. Like someone got to know the real you, and once they got to know you, they just didn't want to be your friend anymore. That is REALLY, REALLY painful.

This EXACT thing happened to someone in the Bible. King David writes about it in Psalm 55. He starts out by telling us that someone is NOT being very kind to him. He says, "*Listen to my prayer, O God. Do not ignore my cry for help! Please listen and answer me, for I am overwhelmed by my troubles. My enemies shout at me, making loud and wicked threats. They bring trouble on me and angrily hunt me down.*" (Psalm 55:1-3) King David is NOT having a good day.

But as we look further on in the chapter, we see WHO the person is who is giving him such a hard time! "*This isn't the neighborhood bully mocking me—I could take that. This isn't a foreign devil spitting invective—I could tune that out. It's you! We grew up together! You! My best friend! Those long hours of leisure as we walked arm in arm, God a third party to our conversation.*" (Psalm 55:12-14 MSG)

It's someone who used to be his friend! His best friend!! Can you imagine how sad King David must have felt! The person causing him so much trouble was actually someone who was supposed to be a friend?!

If you have a person who used to be your friend who is now being mean to you, I am really, really sorry, I know that is very hard and I am sorry that this has happened to you. But, you can do exactly what King David did! He asked God to help him. Psalm 55: 16 says, "*But I will call on God, and the Lord will rescue me.*" Ask God to help you know what to do in the situation. Maybe you need to apologize for something. Maybe you need to reach out to them in kindness. Or maybe you just need to let it go and ask God to help you forgive the person who has hurt you.

Man, it's **SO** hard to forgive the people that hurt us. It's hard to let go when everything in us wants to fight back and make them hurt the way we are hurting. But God wants you to forgive others. Colossians 3:13 says, *"Make allowance for each other's faults, and forgive anyone who offends you. Remember, the Lord forgave you, so you must forgive others."*

Ask God to help you let go of your hurt and anger. Ask Him to help you forgive.

What if you and I decided that we were going to just STOP all the mean girl stuff. What if we just said, "You know what, I will just choose to be a kind girl." If we chose to forgive and love those who hurt us, and always show love and stick up for the girls who are being hurt by other people, we could really change a lot of things.

SO – let's do it! No more mean.

In your Polka Dot Spot section, you will find the Polka Dot Girls NO MORE MEAN Treaty. It simply says this:

"I promise, as Polka Dot Girl and as a daughter of God, to treat other girls with kindness and respect. I will not be mean. I will not Do Drama. And I will forgive and love those who are mean to me, instead of being mean back. I will show the love of Jesus in the way I talk, act, and treat my friends."

If you want to be a girl who shows love and kindness instead of being mean, sign it and take the pledge!

Closing Prayer: *Dear God, I thank you that you have promised to always be with me no matter what I am going through. I pray you help me know what to do when other girls are being mean to me. I pray you help me to "Don't Do Drama" and to forgive and love those who are mean to me. And I promise that I will be kind and loving to the girls around me, because it will make you happy. I love you, Amen.*

Have you ever had someone be mean to you? How did that make you feel?

Have you ever wanted to be mean back to someone who was mean to you? What does God say we should do?

In this lesson we learned to "Don't Do Drama!" What does that mean? In the spaces below, write out some things you can say to your friend to help calm down the drama!

I'm sorry you are upset, can we talk about this?

week 8

What should we do if we are being bullied by someone?

What does it mean to love your enemies?

Write the names of some people who haven't been very nice to you and then write a prayer next to their name asking God to bless them.

_____ Prayer:
   Name

_____ Prayer:
   Name

_____ Prayer:
   Name

Have you ever had someone who used to be your friend, suddenly become mean and not want to be your friend anymore? How did that make you feel?

God says that we need to forgive the friends who hurt us. Color in the letters of our theme verse: "*Love your enemies! Do good to those who hate you. Bless those who curse you. Pray for those who hurt you.*" – Luke 6:27-28

147

No More Mean Treaty

Instructions:

- Carefully tear out the Polka Dot Girl No More Mean Treaty.
- Color the treaty.
- Sign it!
- Mount the treaty onto pretty paper of your choice.
- Attach ribbon on the back of the treaty with masking tape.
- Hang the signed treaty in your room to remind yourself to follow the Polka Dot Girl No More Mean Treaty!

I promise, as a **Polka Dot Girl**

and as a **daughter** of God,

to treat other girls with **kindness** and **respect**.

I will **not be mean!**

I will **not Do Drama!**

And I will **forgive** and **love** those who are mean to me,
instead of being mean back.

I will show the **love** of Jesus in the way
I talk, act, and **treat** my friends.

Signed by: _____

Date: _____

Activity Sheets

What should you do when we're in a situation where it seems like there is **LOTS** of drama and fighting and maybe even someone picking on us for no reason? The following scripture instructs us how to treat people who hurt us.

Step 1: Find the hidden words from the list in the Word Search Puzzle.

Step 2: Place the hidden words in the correct blank in the scripture verse.

Step 3: Go to your Bible and find Luke 6:27-28 NLT to check your answer.

"_____ your enemies! Do _____

to those who hate you. _____ those who curse you.

_____ for those who hurt you." – Luke 6:27-28 NLT

WORD SEARCH PUZZLE

N	O	O	T	B	B
V	T	A	F	M	L
P	E	E	G	U	E
R	S	F	O	V	S
A	F	S	O	X	S
Y	D	L	D	M	T

WORD LIST

bless   *love*   *good*   *pray*

Jesus died on the cross so that the sins of all people could be forgiven. He did this out of love.

Solve the puzzle to find out what God wants us to do for the people who have hurt us.

___ ___ ___ ___ 6:26-27 NLT

Answer: "*Love your enemies! Do good to those who hate you. Bless those who curse you. Pray for those who hurt you.*" Luke 6:26-27 NLT

Look up the Bible passages below and fill in the blank lines with the missing letters.

When you have filled in all the blank lines, put the circled letters in the matching numbered lines to find out what God wants us to do for the people who have hurt us. All scripture NIV

"A fool gives full ____ ____ ____ ____ to his anger, but a wise man keeps himself

3   15

under control." – Proverbs 29:11

"Do to ____ ____ ____ ____ ____ ____ as you would have them do to you." – Luke 6:31

2

"But I ____ ____ ____ ____ to God, and the ____ ____ ____ ____ saves me."

1   7

– Psalm 55:16

"Bear with each other and ____ ____ ____ ____ ____ ____ ____ whatever

12 13   4,17

grievances you may have against one another. Forgive as the Lord forgave you."

– Colossians 3:13

"And when you stand ____ ____ ____ ____ ____ ____ ____, if you hold

8   5,10   6

anything against anyone, forgive him, so that your Father in heaven may forgive you your sins." – Mark 11:25

"Lord, how many times shall I forgive ____ ____

18

____ ____ ____ ____ ____ ____ ____ *when he sins against me? Up to seven times?"*

9,14   16

Jesus answered, "I tell ____ ____ ____, not seven times, but seventy-seven times."

11

– Matthew 18:21-22

WORD LIST

you	*others*	*praying*	*call*
vent	*brother*	*forgive*	*my*
Lord			

God's instruction is to:

____ ____ ____ ____   ____ ____ ____   ____ ____ ____ ____

  1   2   3   4   5   6   7   8   9   10   11

____ ____ ____   ____ ____ ____ ____.

  12   13   14   15   16   17   18

Weekly Challenge

Grow – Grow by reading the story of King David in Psalm 55.

Love – Practice loving your enemies this week. Each night, say a prayer for someone who has been mean to you. Pray for God to bless them.

Act – Practice "Don't Do Drama!" When you are with your friends, refuse to get let things get ugly. Practice talking through your problems without getting too upset.

Memorize – Memorize the theme verse:

"Love your enemies! Do good to those who hate you. Bless those who curse you. Pray for those who hurt you."
Luke 6:27-28

Relationships

Do The Right Thing

WHAT'S THE POINT?
GOD WANTS YOU TO STAND UP FOR WHAT IS RIGHT.

theme verse

"Do what is right. Then you will be accepted. If you don't do what is right, sin is waiting at your door to grab you. It longs to have you. But you must rule over it."
Genesis 4:7 NIRV

related bible story

King Josiah
2 Kings 22

We have talked this entire series about how important our relationships are. God has blessed us with incredible friends and family who walk through our lives with us. They remind us that we are not alone and they can help us become the very best we can be!

But sometimes our relationships can become so important to us that we are willing to do anything to make the people in our lives happy.

Sophia loved spending time with her friends. One day, she was at the store with her friend Carmen. Suddenly, she saw Carmen take a piece of candy from the shelf and put it in her pocket without paying for it. Sophia couldn't believe it!

157

Then it got worse. Carmen took another piece of candy and put it in Sophia's pocket too. Sophia didn't know what to do. She knew that it was wrong to steal, but she didn't want her friend to get mad at her. She didn't say anything and then spent the rest of the day feeling sick to her stomach.

Sometimes our friends try to get us to do things that we know we shouldn't do. Sometimes our friends say things that we know aren't pleasing to God. And sometimes our friends can behave in a way that we KNOW isn't right.

What should we do in those moments? Does a good friend just overlook those things and not say anything? Or does a good friend stand up for what is right?

The answer is ALWAYS that a good friend stands up for what is right. A good friend wants their friends to make right choices and sometimes that means we have to speak up when your friends are doing something that is wrong. And even if that means your friend gets mad at you or EVEN says that they won't be your friend anymore, it is better for you to do what is right.

POLKA DOT POINTERS

If someone tells you that they aren't going to be your friend anymore if you don't do what they tell you – even if it's something you don't want to you or something you know is wrong – then that person isn't a very good friend. GOOD friends don't make other people do things they know are wrong. And good friends always help you make good choices, not bad ones. Make sure you surround yourself with good friends!

But this can be REALLY hard! Reeeeeeallllyyy hard. No one likes to have their friends upset with them. It's not easy to speak up when everyone else is just going along with what is going on. And it is very hard to stand up and do what is right when everyone else is doing what is wrong.

But God always wants you to do the right thing. He asks us to stand up and not just go along with the things our friends are doing that we know are wrong. 1 Peter 3:14 says, *"But even if you suffer for doing what is right, God will reward you for it. So don't worry or be afraid of their threats."* Even when we are scared of what our friends might say, we need to honor God by doing what is right.

How do we do this? How can we get the courage to do the right thing even when we feel HUGE pressure to just go along with what everyone else is doing?

First of all, we need to

➡ 1. Live to please God.

Sophia really liked her friend Carmen. She always sat with her at lunch and walked home from school with her. Sophia hated the idea of Carmen being mad at her and she couldn't imagine what it would be like if Carmen wouldn't be her friend.

But in her heart, she knew that what Carmen was doing was wrong. She knew that she shouldn't take things that she hadn't paid for and that it wouldn't please her parents and especially that it wouldn't please God.

But the problem was that Sophia was more worried about what her FRIEND would think than what GOD would think. She was more worried about making her FRIEND happy than making GOD happy. She didn't want her FRIEND to be upset with her, but she wasn't so worried about making GOD upset that she didn't steal the candy. Proverbs 29:25 says, *"Fearing people is a dangerous trap, but to trust in the Lord means safety."*

What would have given Sophia the courage to do the right thing? She should have been more worried about pleasing GOD than pleasing her friend. Even though she was scared that her friend would be mad at her, she should have been MORE concerned with doing something that God says is wrong.

Girls, we **HAVE** to care more about what God thinks than **ANYONE ELSE.** We have to do the things that will make **HIM** happy even if it means our friends might be upset with us. Choosing the right thing always pleases God. And we have to live to please God instead of pleasing other people.

The times when we fail to stand up for what is right, we are usually more concerned with pleasing our friends than we are about pleasing God. John 12:43 talks about some people who were having this **EXACT** problem. It says, "*For they loved human praise more than the praise of God.*" People were making wrong choices because they wanted to make people happy **MORE** than they wanted to make God happy.

Make the decision today that you are **ALWAYS** going to do the thing that will please God. Make **HIM** first in your life, and in the moments when you are feeling scared to stand up to your friends, you will **KNOW** in your heart that you **HAVE** to please God more than other people.

Galatians 1:10 says, "*If I were still trying to please men, I would not be Christ's servant.*" Let's be girls who are servants of Christ and live to please **HIM** instead of other people!

The second way we can stand up for what is right is to,

➡ **2. Know what the Bible says, and then DO it!**

There's a story in the Bible about a young man named Josiah. Josiah became the King of Judah when he was 8 years old!! Can you imagine?!? The years before Josiah became King, the other leaders of Judah had decided to walk away from God. They didn't do all the things the Bible told them to do anymore. Actually, Josiah didn't even **KNOW** about the law and the commands of God! His parents hadn't taught Him about the things that God said were right and wrong.

But Josiah had a heart that wanted to please God. One day, Josiah's high priest discovered the scrolls in the Temple that had the laws of God written on them. The high priest told Josiah what the law said and Josiah became very upset because he realized that all the people were not doing the things that God had asked them to do. He said this to the high priest, "*Go to*

the Temple and speak to the Lord for me and for the people and for all Judah. Inquire about the words written in this scroll that has been found. For the Lord's great anger is burning against us because our ancestors have not obeyed the words in this scroll. We have not been doing everything it says we must do." (2 Kings 22:13)

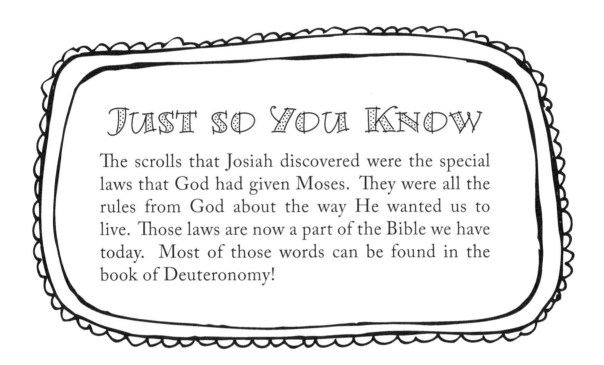

JUST SO YOU KNOW

The scrolls that Josiah discovered were the special laws that God had given Moses. They were all the rules from God about the way He wanted us to live. Those laws are now a part of the Bible we have today. Most of those words can be found in the book of Deuteronomy!

Once Josiah understood the way that God wanted him and all the people of Judah to live, he went to work. He tore down all the idols in the land because the law told him to. He had the people say they were sorry for their behavior, because the scrolls told him to. He made all the changes that the law told him to make because he wanted to honor God. 2 Kings 22:2 says this about Josiah: *"He did what was pleasing in the Lord's sight and followed the example of his ancestor David. He did not turn away from doing what was right."*

If you're going to do the things that God wants you to do, then you need to know the Bible! Josiah wasn't doing the things that God wanted – simply because He didn't know any better! You need to read your Bible and learn the things that God say we should do. And we should also read the Bible to learn the things that God says we shouldn't do!

The Bible is so AMAZING. It can give us wisdom and insight in SO many areas of our lives. It can help us know how to be a kind friend, a good daughter, a hard worker, and many, many other things. 2 Timothy 3:16 says, "*All Scripture is inspired by God and is useful to teach us what is true and to make us realize what is wrong in our lives. It corrects us when we are wrong and teaches us to do what is right.*"

God will show you the right way to live your life through the words He wrote to you in the Bible. BUT- you have to read it and learn what it says!! That's why it's so important to read your Bible every day – so you can know the things God wants you to do!

And the last way you can do the right thing is to

⇨ 3. Be a leader.

When Josiah discovered the law, he quickly changed the things in his own life that weren't pleasing to God. But he did even more than that! He led the other people in his nation back to the ways of God.

God wants you to make the right choices and He wants you to help LEAD other people into the right choices as well. There will come a moment sometime in your life when a group of friends is heading for a wrong choice. Maybe everyone at a slumber party is watching something they shouldn't be watching or a group of friends is being mean to someone. In those moments, you have a choice. You can go along with what everyone else is doing, or you can stand up and be a leader! Instead of following other people down the wrong path, you can stand up and lead your friends down the RIGHT path!

God doesn't want you to follow other people. He wants you to be a leader! He doesn't want you to do whatever other people say, even when you know it's wrong. He wants you to lead your friends into doing the right thing!

There is a verse in Deuteronomy that talks about being a leader. It says, "*If you listen to these commands of the Lord your God that I am giving you today, and if you carefully obey them, the Lord will make you the head and not the tail, and you will always be on top and never at the bottom.*" (Deuteronomy 28:13)

It might sound funny, but when my kids are leaving the house to go play with their friends, do you know what I say to them? I tell them, "You are the head and not the tail." What does that mean? Well, think about a puppy. He's running around all cute and cuddly and wagging his tail.

What is deciding where that puppy is going to go: his head or his tail? His HEAD! What is deciding what that puppy is going to do: his head or his tail? His HEAD. The head is the leader of the dog. The tail just follows behind.

You and I are the head and not the tail! We should be leading our friends into GOOD things, not following our friends into bad things. We should not follow our friends into doing things we know will not please God. We should lead our friends into things that we know are right! YOU are the head and not the tail. You are a leader, not a follower. You can choose the RIGHT thing instead of following people into the wrong thing!!

God wants you to stand up for what is right. Genesis 4:7 says, "*Do what is right. Then you will be accepted. If you don't do what is right, sin is waiting at your door to grab you. It longs to have you. But you must rule over it.*" (NIRV) You have a choice. You can do the right thing – or you can choose the wrong thing. God is there to help you make the right choices and live a life that honors Him.

Closing Prayer: *Dear God. I want to stand up for the right thing. Help me to want to please you more than I want to please my friends. I will read your Word and do the things it tells me to do. And I want to be a leader who shows other people how to honor you. Amen.*

Have you ever had a friend try to get you to do something you knew was wrong? Write out what happened here.

Why is to hard to stand up to our friends when they want us to do something that isn't right?

Does a good friend just overlook things that are wrong and not say anything? Or does a good friend stand up for what is right?

A good friend **ALWAYS** stands up for what is right. Color in the word **ALWAYS** in the sentence below.

A GOOD FRIEND ALWAYS STANDS UP FOR WHAT IS RIGHT.

What does it mean to "live to please God?'

What are some things you can do to "live to please God" instead of living to please your friends? Be specific.

King Josiah learned what the Bible said and then worked hard to follow the things it told him to do. Is there something you have worked hard to do (or stop doing) because the Bible told you to?

The Bible says that "you are the head and not the tail." What does that mean?

Polka Dot Plus

Activity Sheets

Deuteronomy 28:13 NLT talks about being a leader. It says, "*If you listen to these commands of the Lord your God that I am giving you today, and if you carefully obey them, the Lord will make you the HEAD and NOT the TAIL, and you will always be on top and never at the bottom.*"

Color the puppy below and remember that it's his head that decides where he wants to go and what he wants to do. The head is the leader of the dog. His tail just follows behind.

The Bible is so AMAZING. It can give us wisdom and insight in SO many areas of our lives. God will show you the right way to live your life through the words He wrote to you.

Unscramble the words below, place them in the correct part of the scripture verse and discover what God has to say about leadership!

Step 1: Unscramble the words.

wflloo   ___ ___ ___ ___ ___ ___

ltia   ___ ___ ___ ___

dhae   ___ ___ ___ ___

mmcadsno   ___ ___ ___ ___ ___ ___ ___ ___

dLro   ___ ___ ___ ___

tbtomo   ___ ___ ___ ___ ___ ___

Step 2 - Fill in the blanks of the scripture verse below with the correct unscrambled word from step one.

The LORD will make you the ___ ___ ___ ___,

not the ___ ___ ___ ___.

If you pay attention to the ___ ___ ___ ___ ___ ___ ___ ___

of the ___ ___ ___ ___ your God that I give you this day and carefully

___ ___ ___ ___ ___ ___ them, you will always be at the top, never

at the ___ ___ ___ ___ ___ ___.

Step 3 – Check your answer by reading Deuteronomy 28:13 NIV.

WORD LIST

Lord   *tail*   *bottom*   *commands*   *follow*   *head*

God is there to help you make the right choices and live a life that honors him.

Step 1: Read each verse below and fill in the blank. All scripture NIV.

"But even if you should _____ for what is right, you are blessed. Do not fear what they fear; do not be frightened." – 1 Peter 3:14

"Fear of man will prove to be a snare, but whoever _____ in the LORD is kept safe." –Proverbs 29:25

"If you do what is right, will you not be _____? But if you do not do what is right, sin is crouching at your door; it desires to have you, but you must master it." – Genesis 4:7

"Am I now trying to win the approval of men, or of God? Or am I trying to please men? If I were still trying to please men, I would _____ be a servant of Christ." – Galatians 1:10

"He did what was right in the eyes of the LORD and walked in all the ways of his father _____, not turning aside to the right or to the left." – 2 Kings 22:2

"All Scripture is God-breathed and is _____ for teaching, rebuking, correcting and training in righteousness." – 2 Timothy 3:16

"...for they loved _____ from men more than praise from God." – John 12:43

Step 2: Circle the first letter of each missing word from above, and put that letter into the blank spaces below to find out what God wants you to do!

God wants you to _____ _____ _____ _____ _____   _____ _____!

Word List

David	*praise*	*useful*	*accepted*
suffer	*trusts*	*not*	

Weekly Challenge

Grow – Grow by reading the story of King Josiah in 2 Kings 22.

Love – Be a good friend by helping your friends make the right choices. Speak up even when it's hard and love them even if they get angry with you for doing what is right.

Act – Read your Bible this week and write down some of the things that God says. Start in the book of Proverbs, it is full of wisdom for how to live our lives in a way that pleases God!

Memorize – Memorize the theme verse.

"Do what is right. Then you will be accepted. If you don't do what is right, sin is waiting at your door to grab you. It longs to have you. But you must rule over it."

Genesis 4:7 NIRV

CPSIA information can be obtained
at www.ICGtesting.com
Printed in the USA
LVHW061230030619
619963LV00005B/879/P